MODERN
PAINT
EFFECTS

MODERN PAINT EFFECTS

A guide to contemporary paint finishes from inspiration to technique

ANNIE SLOAN

FIREFLY BOOKS

A FIREFLY BOOK

First printing

U.S. Cataloging-in-Publication Data
Sloan, Annie
Modern paint effects : a guide to contemporary paint finishes from
inspiration to technique/Annie Sloan. —1st ed.
[128] p. : col. ill. ;   cm.
Includes index.
Summary: Faux painting techniques to create contemporary
finishes for the home.
ISBN 1-55209-490-1 (bound)
ISBN 1-55209-488-X (pbk.)
1. Painting -- Techniques. 2.Wood finishing.
I. Title.
745.723 –dc21   2000   CIP

Canadian Cataloguing in Publication Data
Sloan, Annie, 1949-
Modern paint effects : a guide to contemporary paint finishes from
inspiration to technique
Includes index
ISBN 1-55209-490-1 (bound)
ISBN 1-55209-488-X (pbk.)
1. House painting. 2. Interior decoration. I. Title.
TT385.S562 2000   698'.1'028   c99-933093-4

First published in the United States in 2000 by
Firefly Books (U.S.) Inc.
P.O. Box 1338, Ellicott Station
Buffalo, New York, 14205

First published in Canada in 2000 by
Firefly Books Ltd.
3680 Victoria Park Avenue
Willowdale, Ontario, M2H 3K1

Conceived, edited and designed by Collins and Brown Limited.

Editors: Claire Waite, Alison Wormleighton
Designer: Jonathan Raimes
Photographer: Tino Tedaldi
Picture Researcher: Philippa Lewis

Reproduction by Hong Kong Graphic and Printing Ltd
Printed and bound by Sing Cheong Printing Co. Ltd, Hong Kong

Contents

Introduction

Paint is today's essential home accessory. More and more designer paint ranges are being launched, and a wonderful array of innovative new products is available now, from pearlized paints to colored plaster. Knowing how to make the most of these provides the quickest and easiest way to upgrade your home. Whether you prefer richly subtle shades or excitingly vibrant colors, velvety flat finishes or colorful pattern, there are many exciting new ways you can personalize your surroundings.

This book explores the decorative potential of the latest paint techniques, products and trends, bringing interior decoration with paint right up-to-date. The paint effects are grouped into two sections. The first covers textured effects using the latest paints and colored plaster, while the second comprises modern approaches to pattern.

As well as detailed step-by-step instructions for using the new products and techniques, there are specially commissioned photographs showing each finished effect, and suggestions for innovative variations on that technique. In addition, there is guidance on finding inspiration for your own ideas and then translating your ideas into paint. Each paint effect in the book is compared with similar effects found in nature, textiles, art, architecture–even manufacturing and electronics. By becoming aware of the similarities, you will develop an "eye" that will enable you to use the textures and patterns all around you as inspiration for original designs of your own.

In our homes we are now surrounded by new, high-tech materials and designs, not only found in the latest gadgets but also introduced by architects and designers. Only equally modern paint finishes can live up to them, and fortunately technology has obliged, with a wonderful array of brilliant new products, including sparkle, pearlized, and metallic paints and polished plaster.

Opposite: Modern design and decoration is more likely to express and reflect individual attitudes to life, rather than conforming to one ideal. A room may have simple yet exuberant brushstrokes in reflective shiny colors, be meditative and serene, or humming with activity.

Paradoxically, our homes have become refuges from the fast pace and pressures of modern living. As a result, peaceful, uncluttered, minimalist homes, often influenced by Eastern design, have become popular. In minimalist interiors, texture is all the more important, and this is another reason the latest paint finishes look so good in the modern home.

The basic textures of nature, whether in the veins of a leaf or in the layers of a rock, are admired—and emulated using paint effects. Materials that were once dressed and covered are now left unadorned and raw, to be seen as they are. Simple woods, undressed stone, metal girders, and bare concrete all make frequent appearances in contemporary homes.

Nature has, of course, been an inspiration to designers since time immemorial. In the past, however, this involved only what the eye could see, whereas the advent of sophisticated telescopes and microscopes revealed patterns that were previously invisible to the naked eye. For example, molecules and cells, the most basic units of life, were found to be made up of dots, chains, and grid patterns. At the opposite extreme, pictures brought back from space show us other galaxies, nebulae, and comets. Space travel and aerial photography have also provided a dramatically different way of viewing our own landscape.

Opposite and far right: Natural materials can be matte in texture, like the basket and grainy stoneware (right) or shiny, like the magnolia leaf. When there is little pattern, as is the style chosen for many modern interiors, a combination of textures is what makes a room interesting. Many modern paint and building materials have a raw, undressed feel to them, in keeping with the exposed bareness of many of the influences from technology. This computer circuit board is full of shiny color, offbeat lines, and regular squares, all aspects of a different type of influence on modern pattern-making and textural ideas.

Left and above: Images like these, the Milky Way (left) and an aerial shot of a river (above), both the result of developing technologies, have given us a new perspective on our lives, obliquely affecting our ideas about design, color, and decoration.

Science has indeed opened up hidden worlds—not just in nature but also in electronics, engineering, and manufacturing—giving us some astounding new images. And whether it is the structure of a benzene crystal, the pattern formed by a silicon circuit, or the shape of a spiral galaxy, modern architects, designers, artists, photographers, and filmmakers have drawn inspiration from them. Now we are using these designs in our living and working environments, and they, in turn, can be yet another source of inspiration for pattern in the home.

Whereas classical design has always been formal, symmetrical, and orderly, modern design tends to be informal, asymmetrical, random, and quirky. Self-expression is valued in modern art, which means that more expressive brushmarks are acceptable in paintings. Advertising and images from pop culture can be cool and slick—or outrageous, shocking, colorful, and kitsch. All of these approaches have relevance for interior decorating today, and with this book you will learn how to draw inspiration from them and use the latest paint effects to bring contemporary color, texture, and pattern into your home.

USING PAINT & PLASTER

10

Matte paint

Matte is the desert dryness of chamois leather and sand, the chalkiness of charcoal and powdery pastel drawings, of blackboard smudges and soot. It is the smooth, bleached surface of driftwood; the dry, unglazed texture of bisque pottery; the bare, flat finish of concrete; the rough graininess of sandstone.

Mellow and relaxing

A natural matte finish, whether in adobe walls or in soft cotton, linen or canvas fabrics, looks as comfortable and mellow as an old armchair. Lacking any hint of shine or artifice, it has the reassuring quality of the completely natural. It has a velvety and sensual texture, like peach skin or blotting paper, that makes you want to touch it and hold it.

Matte finishes are absorbent, which means that light is soaked up rather than being bounced back, creating a restful, peaceful atmosphere. In white or pale colors, most things that are matte look dusty, powdery, and chalky, but when the colors are dark, they look as soft and rich as velvet. As matte finishes do not demand attention, they are unpretentious and low-key, which makes them perfect for a bedroom or a relaxing sitting room.

Clockwise from top left:
BARE CONCRETE
A slab of reinforced concrete has become an ubiquitous part of our city landscape. It has a bare, dry, utilitarian beauty. Reproduce this look and feel using matte paint with a long-pile roller.

CHALK AND VELVET
Chalky lime paint colored with bright pigments gives a velvet smooth look to the walls in this Marrakech market. Matte colors are often cool, muted and dry looking, such as smoky gray, biscuit brown and dusty khaki. Such quiet colors work best without shine, to attract less attention.

SAND DRY
Sand is dry as a bone but absorbent like blotting paper, becoming darker when wet. It is soft, rounded and quiet, and can be marked and shaped easily with footprints or tires. The same qualities are true of matte paint: use an eraser or the end of a paintbrush to incise patterns in wet paint (see page 100).

SOFT PAINT
Soft matte paint can be washed or scrubbed back quite easily, to make a painterly texture. Here, reinforcement rings masked out some of the orange and blue paint, which was also wiped back in places when almost dry.

"When the colors are dark, matte finishes look as soft and rich as velvet"

Using matte paint

Like common matte materials such as cement, adobe, slate, plain wood, linen, and canvas, a matte-painted surface has an unassuming character, and because it absorbs both sound and light, it is the perfect material to use when creating a peaceful, restful interior.

Milk paint, cascin paint, and fresco painting are similar in look and feel to modern matte paints, and to successfully create peaceful surroundings you may want to refer to the colors traditionally made from these natural mediums.

Matte water-based paints have a low plastic content, which means they can be lightly rubbed back with a damp cloth or sponge when just dry. They are also ideal colorants for glazes (see page 121) and absorb furniture wax beautifully, giving a smooth, mellow finish. For a powdery finish, choose pale colors or white, but for a soft, velvet look, pick out darker shades.

Opposite: The flat quality of matte black paint makes it an effective alternative to a blackboard. Here, a panel of matte black paint is incorporated into a design consisting of a collection of rectangular shapes of different widths and lengths, painted using a long-pile roller in medium-luster biscuit colors (see page 21) which show the dead flat finish of the black paint to full effect.

2 Using a damp, almost wet sponge rub the surface randomly, in places pleasing to the eye. The paint will come off easily. Wash out the sponge when it becomes saturated with paint and continue rubbing back until the desired finish is attained.

1 Apply the paint using a brush or roller, allowing for a liberal but even distribution. Leave the coat for approximately five to ten minutes until barely dry.

More ideas

Matte paint is particularly useful when executing decorative techniques because it has a soft, flexible consistency. It can be washed off gently in places while still a little wet – it will dry to a very hard, almost plaster-like finish after a few days – which makes it a good candidate for incising techniques. Before the paint dries, work a brush or other implement into the paint to produce a specific texture. Matte paint is also a very good material to use with the frottage technique (see page 112), since its low plastic content stops the newspaper sticking to it and leaving newsprint behind.

The flat quality of matte paint provides the perfect contrast to metallic, pearlized, and glossy translucent paints and can be used alongside them for dramatic impact.

Left: Matte paint is absorbent, which means that the application of varnish (see page 122) causes it to darken in color. Use a roller to apply matte water-based varnish over a mid-blue matte-painted wall, to produce stripes with organic, rough edges (see page 62). Create thin, subtle cream lines using the edge of cardboard and a medium-luster paint (see pages 21 and 78).

Left: This wall has a very soft, fabric-like look that works wonderfully with natural, bleached wood. Over a sea blue matte base coat, apply a coat of pale blue matte paint. When the paint is still a little damp, wet a sponge and use it to wash off some of the paint in stripes, working mostly downward but with the occasional horizontal swipe. Let the water from the sponge dribble down the wall making running rivulet marks— cover the floor with cloth or newspaper to absorb the water as you work.

Left: The blue chosen for the wall of this kitchen is a strong, vibrant color, but because it is in the form of a matte paint the effect is soft and undemanding. Paint matte blue over a yellow medium-luster base coat (see page 21) and leave to dry. Rub back the blue with coarse sandpaper, allowing the yellow to show through in a random pattern.

Above: To achieve a texture similar to that of a weather-bleached pebble, apply a chalk-colored matte paint over gray. Then randomly wash off the barely-dry paint in places, using a damp sponge.

Medium-luster paint

Clockwise from top left:
PORCELAIN GLAZE
Porcelain, originally from the East, introduced a range of new and stunning colors to the West, including celadon green, tomato red, aubergine, and imperial yellow. The glaze used on porcelain has a soft shine, and the fine opacity of the finish gives colors character and directness. Modern paint production methods make it possible to recreate this finish in the same wide choice of colors.

SENSUAL SHEEN
Satin, made by weaving silk in a particular way, has a weight and soft roundness to the folds that is unique. The fabric has a sensual, gentle sheen and a hint of nostalgic Hollywood glamor. Frottage two medium-luster paints in colors of similar tone to reproduce the same loose drapery look (see page 112).

BURNT CHARCOAL
The shiny smoothness of a log burned to charcoal has a dark, almost lustrous depth. As the light catches the charcoal it displays a soft, leathery sheen. A dark blue medium-luster paint could replicate the look, perhaps enhanced with a crackle varnish filled with black oil paint (see page 116).

GENTLE COLOR
Two medium-luster paints can be lightly rollerpainted one over the other to make light, watery looking colors (see page 115).

Like porcelain or bone china, this paint has a delicate sheen. Whether dark like a piece of slate or creamy white like the shell of an egg, it looks as though it has been lightly polished. It is as silken-smooth to the touch as a slab of marble. This paint has a feeling of elegance—not as assertive and urban as glossy paint, nor as natural and relaxed as matte paint, but with a refined look about it. The gentle sheen of the paint reflects light into a room, in much the same way as light falls on ivory, glazed cotton, silk, or waxed wood, creating a defined shadow that adds depth to a room.

Elegant but tough

The elegant appearance of medium-luster paint, also known as semi-gloss paint, belies its strength. It is tough, durable and flexible, hence its popularity, and is suitable for walls, woodwork and furniture. For a refined, sophisticated look, use it on walls and woodwork together; or for a more mellow look, apply it just to the woodwork. The precise look and feel of this paint varies, depending on the manufacturer. Because of its popularity, it is available in a huge array of colors.

"The gentle sheen of this paint reflects light into a room"

Using medium-luster paint

Medium-luster paints–sometimes also known as semi-gloss paints– can be bought with differing degrees of "sheen": they may be as shiny and smooth as porcelain, as soft as satin or, like eggshell paints, appear closer to a matte look and feel.

This type of paint comes in a huge variety of colors, from all the pale neutrals to brilliant shocking hues. It can be used as flat color, is a good choice as a base coat to colored glazes (see page 121), and is effective on walls, woodwork and furniture. Before choosing a medium-luster paint, remember that, as the light catches the surface, the slight sheen in the paint will show up any imperfections.

Apply medium-luster paints with a roller over the main part of a wall and use a small brush to reach the edges and more intricate areas. Spread the paint out well, applying two even layers where necessary, rather than one thick one. Two coats will probably be needed when covering a dark color with a lighter shade.

Above: Medium-luster paints are available in a multitude of mouthwatering colors, often chosen because they have a similar "flavor." When seen together, perhaps on a color chart, or grouped in pots as here, who can fail to be tempted?

1 Apply the paint with a roller, either long-pile or sponge, taking care to spread it out evenly. Do not apply it too thickly or allow the roller to become saturated in paint, as this will cause the paint to spray out and may leave bubbles in the finish.

Opposite: The simple, rough-edged square design on this bedroom wall was inspired by the work of modern artists who explore color by applying it in large, bold slabs. Use a long-pile roller to apply light brown medium-luster paint over an off-white medium-luster base. The gentle sheen in the paints emphasizes the undulating nature of this old wall.

More ideas

The practicality of medium-luster paint makes it a very popular and frequently used medium. Buy tester pots to use on small projects, or work with paint left over from previous decorating jobs. These paints can be used for almost all of the pattern-making techniques in this book. I like to use it as the base coat for glaze techniques, because its non-absorbent properties help to slow down the glaze drying time. You can also use medium-luster paints with a little added glaze (see page 121) to paint offbeat brushmarks, incise motifs, and produce patination effects such as a colorwash or frottage finish (see pages 96, 100, 108 and 112).

Left: Both the top and legs of this modern cube table were given a textured surface treatment, with the medium-luster finish of the top complemented by the high-gloss legs. First of all, I removed the glass top which was replaced later when the decoration was completely dry. Then, over the white base, I painted a rough-edged panel using a roller (see page 115), first in turquoise-blue and then, when the first coat was dry, with a deep blue. On the legs, I began by applying a coat of black glossy translucent paint (see page 26). When dry, I applied copper metallic paint (see page 33), scrubbing the paint on with a brush, to produce a loose texture.

Right: Free-flowing doodles executed through patches of vibrant-colored medium-luster paint make a strong decorative statement on this clear bowl. Apply patches of medium-luster paint in various bright colors to the inside of the bowl. While the paint is still a little wet, use the end of a thin paintbrush to incise a pattern of swirls and loops (see page 100). When the paint is completely dry, apply a layer of black medium-luster paint to the inside of the bowl: a dramatic contrast to the multicolored first coat which will be visible from the outside, through the incised pattern.

Right: I chose to paint the panels on this door with thick coats of medium-luster paint in four ice-cream colors of similar tones that have the same degree of lightness and are pleasing to the eye when placed together. I then painted the rest of the door in a light medium-luster color, ensuring that the central panels remain the focus. Medium-luster paints are a practical solution for a door that is in constant use, since they can be wiped and washed frequently.

Glossy translucent paint

The glossy finish is emphatically modern. From mirror-glass windows, Lucite furniture and shiny cars to PVC, Lycra, and lipgloss, shine has a contemporary glamor and allure. Glossy translucent paint is as shiny and translucent as children's fruit gums, and hard candies, yet when the light shines through, it can take on the quality of a stained-glass window.

Gloss paints work best in bold, positive colors that are strong, clear, and uncomplicated, like those of everyday plastics and modern packaging–brilliant red, strong yellow, and neon blue. If paint colors could talk, these would be shouting.

Layers of translucent color

Painting with this material is like dressing your home in translucent layers of brightly colored silk veils. Modern artists have used this same type of paint, gloss and enamel, to create large, abstract fields of color. As the colors are overlaid, new colors appear–red over black becomes a deep burnt orange, while red over blue becomes purple. By using two colors to create these deep shades, the painted finish has the glowing depth and intensity of an inky-blue lake.

Use this shiny paint in a room and the walls will reflect color as the light bounces off the paint like a mirror, making the room come alive. Paint a color over a white base and the white will radiate through the paint to make it glow with light. The final look is outgoing, gregarious and optimistic.

Clockwise from top left:
CANDY-COATED
The shiny colors of eye-catching gaudy candy for children inspire similar design ideas for a wall. Overlap stencils using the bright glossy translucent colors, or apply the paints with the involuntary dash of a brushstroke (see pages 77 and 96).

SOFTENED FOCUS
I painted this chair seat with red and then yellow glossy translucent paints to make an impressionistic and intense design. The brushmarks remain evident, helping to make the hard, square design softer and giving focus to the chair.

NATURAL SHINE
Shiny textures are usually associated with industrial or processed finishes, but the yellow-greens, brilliant emeralds, and deep bottle greens of glossy leaves provide inspiration for a natural look with the same intense sheen.

FANTASTIC PLASTIC
Shiny black plastic wound tightly around hay takes on a silvery sheen in the sunlight. Use black glossy translucent paint with metallic paints to produce a similar effect, emphasizing the sheen throughout (see page 33).

"Bright, shiny and translucent, like children's fruit gums."

"If paint colors could talk, these would be shouting"

Using glossy translucent paint

To achieve this very shiny translucent look, a semi-opaque, water-based gloss paint is used. If this is difficult to find, use a colored varnish with extra color added, in the form of gloss paint or colorizer, for strength and depth.

    The best way to use the paint is to brush it on with a bristle brush, but one that is not hard or too scratchy. Apply the paint with a sponge roller for a very thin layer, but since the paint dries quickly, overlapping areas may leave a patterned texture. Diluting the paint with a tiny amount of water will allow it to dribble over a flat surface. To ensure it adheres properly, apply this paint over a matte paint base coat (see page 14).

Below: Very shiny paints work best when they are unashamedly bright, but by overlapping colors you can create more subtle shades. Lay and overlap two or more layers of glossy translucent paint, but remember that too many layers can result in muddy colors.

1 Apply the paint using a brush with firm but soft bristles that are not liable to scratch the surface. Spread the paint out and finish by working with just the tip of the brush to lightly blend the paint and remove brush-strokes. Leave to dry.

2 When the first coat is barely dry it is ready for a second coat, even though it may not be completely "cured." Apply the paint as before, spreading it over the first coat to achieve a new color, depth and intensity. If you intend to allow some of the first color to show, start applying the second coat in the central overlapping area and work out to the edge where the two colors meet. This allows all brushstrokes to be feathered out.

Opposite: The distinct architectural shape of this room suggested both the colors and style of decoration for the walls. The idea was inspired by the work of modern abstract artists such as Mark Rothko, who used large slabs of color to create a rich field of consolidated color. I applied two coats of green glossy translucent paint over a matte blue base coat (see page 14), using a brush. I then painted a wide border around the door with yellow glossy translucent paint brushed over the green, feathering gently out to give a softened edge. Over the yellow, turquoise blue was added in random patches to give a rich, slightly uneven overall finish.

Opposite: Build up a pattern on a wall by applying glossy translucent paints with a sponge roller. Roll on random stripes (see page 62) in blue, green, red, and black glossy translucent paints, often overlapping to create new colors. The overpainting makes the colors darker, so those areas not overlapped appear clear and bright.

Left: This whole chest of drawers has been approached as if it were a modern abstract painting. I applied red and yellow glossy translucent paints as rough-edged panels in the center and on top of the piece, while the outer structure I predominantly covered with green and blue glossy translucent paints, with a little red in places. A thin veil of blue was painted over the whole top. The paints were loosely applied using a large, rounded artist's bristle brush and were randomly layered, producing new colors and a rich, painterly effect.

More ideas

Glossy translucent paints have a finish that makes them excellent for combining with other paints to show textural contrast and similarity, yet they are equally effective used alone to produce an enamel-like finish.

Geometric, fluid and offbeat patterns can be reproduced with glossy translucent paints and matte finishes for dramatic effect, or alongside other shiny finishes such as pearlized or metallic paints, which complement each other wonderfully. Glossy translucent paint can also be mixed with glaze and used to give an even more translucent look to frottage or colorwashing techniques, bringing to mind the natural patina of polished stones and shiny leaves, as well as modern fabrics or industrial materials. Adding glaze to the mix also means you have more time to apply the paint before it dries.

Right: I used several coats of pure bright yellow glossy translucent paint on this cupboard to give it a modern look, reminiscent of the shiny lacquer on a yellow car. The panels are emphasized by painting a broad rough swath of white glossy translucent in the recess.

"Metallic paints create clean, sharp lines and hard arrows of light"

Metallic paint

Clockwise from top left:
POWERFUL AND SERENE
A precious golden Buddha, polished with devotion to a gleaming shine, has a comforting serene power. In religious works, gold is not so much a symbol of material value but of spiritual richness. Polish gold paint with the same enthusiasm and devotion.

ARCHITECTURAL PIPEWORK
Metal pipes have a dulled metallic look, serviceable and working rather than bright and luxurious. Texture metallic paint for a similar finish by brushing into it with a bristle brush before it dries.

METALLIC BOWL
Silver and glass have a similar light, delicate look and color and so work well together. To bring out that compatibility I used silver metallic paint on the inside of this glass bowl, incised with a paintbrush (see page 100) and finished with medium-luster silky pastel colors (see page 21).

LIQUID METAL
Sunlight on this lake gives the water a silvery, glassy shine like the scales on a fish's back, and reflections of the sky create metallic blues. The liquid silver water with rounded shapes is soft, cool, and calm. Frottaging silver paint over a mid-toned base coat would have results reminiscent of the scene (see page 112).

There was a time when metal in the home would mean luxurious gold, silver, or pewter, or rustic copper or brass. Now, however, modern industrial metals are used to great effect, not just for small objects but on walls and furniture, too. Modern metals suggest science, technology, space exploration, industry, cars, machinery. Copper pipes and wires, shiny stainless steel, gleaming aluminum, highly polished brass, galvanized metals, and reflective chrome, as well as silver foil, glinting kitchen utensils, and shiny metallic chocolate wrappers all take their place in modern life.

Practicality... or sheer fantasy

The metallic finish combines the clean, scientific, practical approach with a futuristic fantasy, making it a material that can be used in diverse ways. Walls might imitate riveted dulled-metal sheets, tarnished corrugated iron, crumpled silver foil, or smooth polished metals. The effect could be cool and minimalist or a funky riot of color, mixing bright fabrics from India or Mexico, for instance, with shimmering metals.

Metallic paints create clean, sharp lines and hard arrows of light. Using a metallic finish somewhere in a room adds not only brightness but also depth, because the twinned effects of the shininess and the texture of the paint give the eye several planes on which to focus. The textures vary from gleaming, clean and brilliant to lusterless, tarnished, and dulled, while metallic colors are fiery orange, lemon, and mustard yellows, silvery white and dark gray, with dark colors in the shadows.

31

Using metallic paint

There are many metallic paints available on the market, each with their own particular character. Some are quite opaque while others, like the water-based ones used in this book, remain a little translucent. The translucence means that patterns can be made in the paint to give it a textured look.

To ensure good adherence, this paint is best worked over a matte or medium-luster paint (see pages 14–15 and 20–21) rather than a shiny surface. Apply the paint in one of three ways, depending on the desired effect: use a brush over a dark color for a textured finish like the patina found on zinc, or, for a smooth effect, apply with a roller or rub it on with a cloth.

Using a roller

To cover a large area like a wall, it is a good idea to apply metallic paint with a sponge roller. As the paint dries, the roller marks can remain visible in parts so it may be necessary to apply a second coat or, alternatively, use a cloth to rub more paint into the wall around the marked areas.

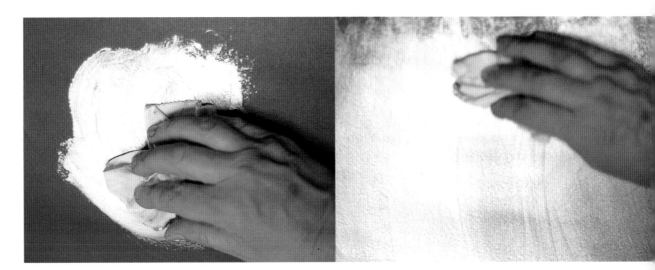

Using a cloth

For a smooth finish, pick up some metallic paint on a soft cotton cloth and rub it into the surface using circular motions. As the paint dries, use the cloth to polish it to obtain a high shine and an even surface. For obvious reasons, this application technique is best executed on small areas.

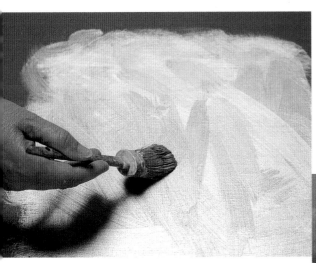

Using a brush

1 Use a brush to apply metallic paint in small sections at a time, to give you time to manipulate it before it dries. Spread the paint out evenly but not too thinly.

2 With a dry, reasonably firm bristle brush, work into the wet paint using small, comma-like motions in both directions to make a cross-hatched effect. The background paint color should be visible through the brushstrokes.

Opposite: In keeping with the clean finishes inherent in this room, the walls are painted to imitate the look of galvanized metal. Bold semi-circles brushed into silver metallic paint, worked over a deep brown matte paint (see page 14), catch the light in places, helping to extend the spatial dimensions of the room.

More ideas

Use metallic paints like any other paints, for flat effects and pattern making, on walls, furniture, or accessories. Silver, gold and copper paints are excellent as base coats to techniques using glaze. Silver in particular radiates plenty of light and acts like a sharp white. Try colorwasing blue over silver, green over copper, and creamy yellow over gold. Alternatively, mix metallic paints with glaze to produce reflective textured finishes.

Remember that these paints work well with most other types of paint: they complement the shiny paints like glossy translucent and pearlized, and contrast effectively with the flat finish of matte paint.

Above: Apply a coat of silver paint to the surface using a sponge roller. Then, use a damp long-pile roller to lightly apply strong orange medium-luster paint (see pages 21 and 115). Randomly vary the pressure you exert on the roller so that the orange is thick in some places and semi-transparent in others, allowing the silver to shine through.

Below: This plain chest of drawers is decorated as a salute to modern metal filing cabinets. Frottage (see page 112) silver metallic paint and glaze over a pale blue base. Leave the newspaper in position a little longer than is strictly necessary, to allow some of the newsprint to transfer onto the surface, so that, in places, reversed black letters are apparent.

Above: This salad bowl, with a beautiful modern shape, has been reinvented with paint. The grain of the wood had opened up with use, making it impractical. First I painted the whole bowl, inside and out, with black glossy translucent paint (see page 26), covering the indented grain of the wood. When dry, I applied silver metallic paint to the inside and the rim, pushing it right into the grooves at the base of the bowl. I then used a cloth to remove the top layer of still-wet paint so that the silver is visible in the grooves but the black shows up elsewhere. To add a little color, red glossy translucent paint was painted like a sash around the outside, making a deep, subtle terracotta over the black.

Above: I particularly liked the uneven texture of this old wall and so chose to highlight it with a reflective paint that catches the light, especially in the evening. For speed, I used a roller to apply the first coat of gold paint. When dry, I rubbed on a second coat of gold paint—with a little copper added for depth—with a soft cloth, polishing it in until dry. On the mantelpiece sits a papier maché bowl that I decorated in the same way using mostly silver paint with a little gold. To soften the edge of the mantelshelf, I rubbed in gold paint with a cloth.

"Pearl combines the smoothness of satin with the color changes of shot silk"

Pearlized paint

The ephemeral quality of pearl is what makes this paint so intriguing. It captures both the subtlety and the excitement of the mother-of-pearl shell, the dragonfly's wing, the hummingbird's plumage. Pearl combines the liquid smoothness of satin with the startling color changes of shot silk. Its opalescent, silvery sheen echoes that of old Roman glass tarnished with time, Italian majolica, mother-of-pearl inlay in furniture, and Victorian lusterware. Opaline pinks, shimmering greens, electric blues, and other luminous hues re-create the iridescent colors that are seen when oil and water come together. The light reflected from the lustrous surface radiates a delicate glow, yet produces colors that are almost neon in their intensity.

Changing light, changing colors

Like its inspiration, the pearl, this paint changes color and quality with the light. Used on walls, it brightens up a room, amplifying naturally occurring light from windows and doors, and artificial light from lightbulbs, but as the light changes through the day, from morning sun to dusk, different effects are created. The intensity of the color also depends on your choice of base. The color of the pearlized paint shines out with dramatic, electric vibrancy when used over a dark, strong base color, while with a light base, the colors will shimmer subtly as the light catches them.

The reflective, glossy finish of pearlized paints makes them similar to metallic paints (see pages 30–35), but softer and gentler in appearance. Because these are new, there are no traditional methods of application, so incorporate them boldly in contemporary designs. And as their strength lies in their ever-changing appearance, use them in places where the fluctuating light can play on the surface to best advantage.

Clockwise from top left:
REFLECTIVE BOWL
A glass bowl provides the perfect base for decoration with pearlized paint: the light will always catch on the round shape and show the finish to full effect. The metal leaf (see page 70) combined in the decoration adds to the effect, emphasizing the pearly flash of the paint. Adhere torn sheets of copper metal leaf to the inside of a glass bowl and paint over them with swirls of blue pearlized paint. When dry, apply a layer of mid-blue matte paint (see page 14).

TWO-TONE SILK
The intensity of color in shot silk changes with the changing light and, in some cases, two complementary colors can be seen, an elusive and ephemeral quality that is echoed in pearlized paint.

BRILLIANT IRIDESCENCE
The iridescent sheen on this car softens the otherwise hard finish and gives depth and brilliance to the color. The pearly finish is like this paint, and suggests femininity and glamor, a diversion from the masculine, practical image the car usually portrays.

PRISM COLORS
Light refracts through the clouds as if they were a prism and makes a pearly rainbow glow in this evening sky. The colors are soft and subtle and yet have a luminous quality, an effect that can be replicated by blending and overlapping the different-colored pearlized paints.

Using pearlized paint

Pearlized paints, like the colors that radiate from the oyster's shell, come in green, blue, and pink, all of which can be overlapped to produce a wealth of original colors.

You can choose to apply these water-based paints thickly or thinly for differing effects. Thickly applied, the paint takes on a whitish sheen when there is no light shining directly on it, and the effect is strong and almost luminous when bathed in light. When a thin layer of paint is applied you will always see the color, whether in direct light or not, but the lit effect is not as strong as it is with the thicker application.

Below: When wet, pearlized paint is opaque and off-white, with just a faint trace of the relevant color. Once it is painted and dried it takes on an almost luminous sheen, tempered by the base. The colors are unmistakable on the black base, but on white the color is much subtler and becomes more and less apparent depending on the light. Here, pearlized paints are shown at their most contrasting; other, less stark backgrounds will cause the paints to have still different effects.

1 Apply pearlized paint with a bristle brush, almost scrubbing the paint on to spread it as far as possible. Here, a black background has been painted with randomly shaped patches of green pearlized paint, and blue patches are being added.

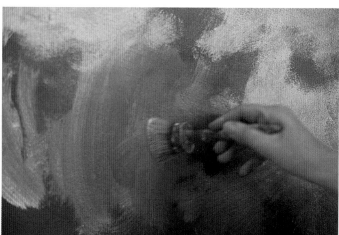

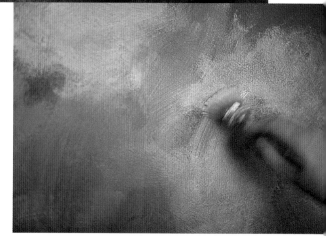

2 Overlap still-wet paints to create new colors. Here, pink pearlized paint is worked into the still-wet blue paint to make a purple hue. When the blue and green are worked together they make a turquoise similar to that seen on the peacock's plumage. Continue working into the paint with the brush until it is dry, "polishing" with the brush to obliterate brushmarks.

Opposite: This small hall in an old country house has light coming at it from several directions, and no electric light of its own. To add interest and bring light to the area, I have used blue pearlized paint in horizontal stripes (see page 61) on a strong matte blue base (see page 14). The focus on the walls changes throughout the day, as light falls on different sections. Two coats were applied using a flat varnish brush to eliminate as many brushmarks as possible, giving a strong, positive pearl effect.

More ideas

Pearlized paint does not dry as quickly as everyday water-based paints, which means it can be manipulated for a short while after it has been applied to make stunning and exciting patterns. Combed, stippled, ragged, and dragged effects can all be tried.

Left: Reminiscent of agate and tiger's eye, the strong irregular stripes on this wall look like striations in rock. Apply green pearlized paint over copper metallic paint (see page 33) and work into the paint with a cardboard comb (see page 59). The application of two reflective paints gives the effect several dimensions that take on varying characteristics depending on how the light falls on the surface.

Below: Red and green are strongly contrasting colors which give this frame a dynamic quality. Apply a coat of green pearlized paint over a matte red base (see page 14) and comb to produce wobbly stripes (see page 58) that, with flashes of brilliance accentuated by natural light, direct the eye to the focus of attention, the picture that they surround.

Opposite: Overlapping pearlized paints create glowing purples and turquoises reminiscent of colors seen in Tiffany glassware. Apply a matte black base coat (see page 14) with a long-pile roller to produce a subtle texture. Then, randomly rub on blue, green, and pink pearlized paints with a brush. Overlap the colors and work the paints in with the brush until dry, in a polishing motion that removes any brushmarks and ensures good coverage.

"Sparkles seem to switch on and off in the light"

Sparkle paint

Clockwise from top left:
CITY NIGHT LIGHTS
Burning dots of light sparkle in a bustling night-time cityscape. Lights blinking, winking, and flashing are never still and extra movement comes from glaring neon signs, traffic lights, and car headlights. Lay sparkle paint on in stripes and blocks for an urban look.

SHOOTING STARS
Firework rockets burst ecstatically, creating showers of sparks shooting high into the sky. The bright red strontium glow illuminates the dark night in a pyrotechnic display so quickly over. Use brushes of different sizes to paint sparkle paint on in lines and spots to achieve the necessary glittery look (see page 96).

WALL SPARKLERS
Red and blue sparkles are painted on in square patches over a wall painted with blue and lilac pearlized paints in loose stripes and patches (see page 38). The two reflective paints complement each other and put on a show of changing colors in the changing light.

MOONLIT WAVES
Close inspection of this seascape reveals a myriad of glinting spots, dots, and dashes of color. The lapping waves of the inky water are caught in the light of the moon, producing a glorious, glittering display. Use sparkle paint over a dotted base coat to remind you of the scene (see page 90).

Sparkles are romantic, dramatic, and alluring. They suggest the glamor and enchantment of the night, and ballgowns glistening with jewels, spangles, and sequins. Lights reflected in water at night are broken up by gentle waves to create twinkling effects. When you fly over a city at night, the colored lights—neon, tungsten, and fluorescent—are clustered in places and then tend to ribbon out along roads. The ultimate sparkles are, of course, the stars in the night sky. Awe-inspiring and mysterious, they form astronomical pictures of the Milky Way and spiral galaxies. By day, you can see sparkles in droplets of water glistening on a windowpane, or in the frost picking out the intricate shape of a spider's web in the sunlight.

Depending on the circumstances and the color combinations, sparkles can be playful and young, flirty and adventurous—or, taken that little bit further, outrageous and flashy. Think firework displays and cheap gaudy toys, garish and exciting.

Catching the light

Sparkles show up best on a dark background but also look good on a light base, where they are less brash and more subtle and delicate. However they are used, they seem to switch on and off as the light catches them. When not in the light, sparkles take on the complementary color of their original hue. So green sparkles can look pink, blue ones can become orange, and gold sparkles turn purple.

Use sparkle paint in a bedroom for glamor, in a child's room for fun, or in a dining room for richness and to add an element of surprise. Transform a bathroom into a room with pizazz. Whichever rooms you use it in, accentuate the sparkles with directional or pinpoint lighting.

Using sparkle paint

The sparkles in this water-based paint are minute specks of glitter held within a liquid which is white when wet but dries to a transparent finish. The color of your base coat is therefore important since it will show through. The base color also affects the intensity of the sparkles, which in turn is affected by the light in the room; you may want to test your ideas on a hidden surface before committing.

When sparkle paint is applied over a dark base, the effect is more pronounced than the subtle effect over a pale color. The paint dries with a shiny finish and a slight roughness to the touch caused by the glitter.

1 Here, green sparkle paint is applied over a dark, purple-plum base to illustrate the paint's maximum impact. A household paintbrush or roller can be used to apply the paint. Spread the paint out as far as possible for a discreet amount of sparkles and take care not to apply it too thickly, since a thick application may not thoroughly dry out and will remain white or translucent.

2 To achieve a very dense layer of sparkles, apply a second or even third coat of paint allowing each layer to dry completely before moving on to the next. Feel free to use the same color or build up layers of different colored sparkle paints for a variety of effects.

Opposite: This intense effect, painted on just one wall of this dining room, is abstractly reminiscent of an urban skyline at night. Over a black glossy translucent base coat (see page 26), apply a single strip of green and a block of red glossy translucent using a roller. Roller strips of sparkle paint in various colors over the black base and green and red blocks (see page 62). Apply several layers of sparkle paint for a vivid effect.

More ideas

Sparkle paint can be used over any other type of paint or decorative technique, from plain matte paint to a two-color stipple or frottage. It is also effective over specific patterns such as stripes or spots, and because of its clear base, acts as a kind of sparkly varnish.

Opposite: Like a phosphorescent midnight sea caught in the moonlight, the decoration in this room takes its cue from the "mermaid" evening dress hanging on the door. Over a warm blue medium-luster paint (see page 21), I applied several layers of blue and green sparkle paint, using a roller.

Above: A single wall in this bedroom is painted with a sparkle effect that gives the room a lift without detracting from the clean look it holds during the day. Randomly attach spotty stickers bought from a stationers across a white wall. Use a roller to paint stripes (see page 62) in shades of blue and green over the stickers, which act as reverse stencils (see page 86). Remove the stickers to reveal playful white dots that break up the stripes and add an extra dimension to the linear effect. Finish by applying two coats of blue sparkle paint with a roller across the whole wall, so that in the gentle night light the wall twinkles and gleams.

Right: This oak tray appears to have had a cast of magical phosphorescent stars sprinkled all over it. To achieve the look, I used three layers of blue and gold sparkle paint applied with a brush. In some lights the sparkles take on different colors.

Polished plaster

Polished plaster has the smooth, even sheen of burnished stones such as agate, alabaster, marble, and basalt–echoes of polished pebbles infinitely varied with texture and color. Like paint, plaster can be colored and marked to imitate a variety of surfaces, from bronze statues to amber beads; the colors are different but they have the same smooth finish. Let nature be your guide when choosing the pigment and method of application. For example, the subtle patches of terracotta-red in the Grand Canyon can be translated into polished plaster. The gentle sweep of tall grasses blown by the wind in a field, or the erratic pattern formed by eddies and swirls on a lake, can be worked into the plaster to give texture. Anything from the uneven speckles on a bird's egg to rusted iron and other industrial textures can be a starting point for plasterwork.

Texture and intense color

The plaster used here is made from a mixture of marble dust, lime, cement, and pigments which, when combined, are manipulated with a trowel onto the surface. Once applied, the plaster is polished using the edge of the trowel. The final effect can be varied in a number of ways. For example, the amount of pigment used, the angle at which the trowel is held, and the length of time the troweling is carried out all help determine whether the finish will be shiny, grainy, or a mixture of both.

Clockwise from top left:
RUST
An old metallic oil tank left outside to rust has blistered and changed color. Streaks of orange and red-brown mingle with specks of pale pink and gray on a background of pinkish-mauve. Use a coarser grain of marble dust to achieve this look, starting with a gray plaster and finishing with a pink plaster top coat.

"NO. 8"
Mark Rothko (1903–70), the American artist, painted layer upon layer of color to achieve astonishing depth and subtlety of color. Here, in a detail of "No. 8" the strength of color and the play of the two tones can be seen. Overlaying colored plaster is a method of achieving that same depth in a way that just can't be done with decorator's paint.

BEACH CONTOURS
The lines of sand on a beach show the tide's movements, a reminder of how far it got before it stopped and ebbed away. Delicate streaks of washed sand and uneven lines map the contours of the beach, providing the inspiration for a textured wall surface.

POLISHED PLASTER BARK
This marmorino effect is reminiscent of dried bark on a tree as uneven textured ridges forge across the wall. The pale orange base layer is smooth and appears in large, dramatic shapes while the uneven streaks of the matte, dark orange top coat are more granular in texture.

"Echoes of polished pebbles infinitely varied with texture and color"

Using polished plaster

This hard, highly polished and very modern–looking plaster finish is a reinterpretation of a very old technique used in various forms from Italy to India. Using marble dust, lime, cement, and water with pigments to color it, the mixture is applied with a metal trowel and worked on until smooth and polished.

3 When the first coat is dry, after about one hour, the process can be repeated for up to three layers.

Opposite: Mix a strong, vibrant green pigment into the plaster and apply it with powerful swipes to achieve the effect of a deep swath of color with bursts of intensity. The look of polished plaster can be as soft and subtle or as wild and vibrant as desired: look carefully at the amount of pigment you use and the way you manipulate the trowel at first application.

2 Load a little of the mixture onto a metal trowel and apply it to the wall, keeping the trowel almost parallel to the surface. Continue in this way, working systematically down the wall.

1 Mix marble dust, lime, and cement in roughly equal measures and then add water until the mixture is the consistency of thick mud. Add pigment, testing the color by wiping a thin layer on some paper and letting it dry. The color will usually be paler when dry than when wet.

4 To produce a shine, work the final coat with the trowel before the plaster has dried. Hold the trowel at a steep angle to the wall and wipe it across the surface to remove the watery top layer. This is known as "skimming the fat" and reveals the aggregate (the marble grains and cement). The remarkable shine that this process produces is caused by the lime in the mixture.

More ideas

Plaster can be used to produce many different looks, achieved by using the basic mixture but with slightly different ingredients and working methods. Different textures can be achieved by using fine, medium, or coarse marble grain and by using different types of troweling techniques, such as varying the angle of the float. The surface may be left pitted, clouded, or speckled or be given an extra degree of shine from very glossy to a softer, more satin effect by polishing or using waxes and varnishes.

Above: This chimney-piece in a house designed by architect Charles Rutherford stands freely like a column, indented with a black-painted fireplace and white-backed display niche. The wall surface has been treated with gray polished plaster to which bronze powders have been added (see page 121).

Opposite: Two layers of blue plaster on this wall create an effect similar to ripples in water. Apply a rough base layer made using coarse grain marble dust, then make a smoother top layer, mixed using a fine grain marble dust, and apply it while the base layer is still slightly damp.

Above right: The bright blue plaster on this wall has a smooth stucco finish and was polished with the trowel until very shiny. The slight texture in the finish is reminiscent of the subtle marks of water on a sandy beach.

Right: Unevenly cover the first layer of matte plaster with later layers of plaster mixed with a coarser marble grain. Polish the final layer with the trowel.

USING PATTERN

54

Clockwise from top left:
DIAGONAL AND FINE
The veins on this leaf are regularly spaced but are thin and uneven, an effect that would look wonderful if enlarged on a wall. Delicate and sensitive lines coursing at different diagonal angles across the surface could be executed in an opaque paint, juxtaposed against a translucent glaze background.

ELECTRIC SHOCK
Each bright plastic-wire stripe is completely independent of the other and makes a hard, solid, positive line, a look that can be successfully transposed to a wall.

ZEN CALM
A series of perfect raked lines encircle and flow smoothly and calmly around the rock in this Zen garden in Japan. The regular lines hold no surprises or harsh movement, an exquisite effect that could be interpreted with paint on walls or furniture, using a comb instead of a rake.

RESTFUL STYLE
Japanese Zen gardens inspired this decoration, where raked sand makes a restful, flowing design. The minimal decoration on this stool was designed to echo that feel, and even though little color is used, a strong overall look is still achieved. The simple lines—curved, waved, and straight—were produced using a graduated comb, making the stripes randomly vary in width, over a base paint the color of unbleached canvas.

FOLDED AND FRACTURED
This magnificent rock formation in the Grand Canyon shows the successive layers of material that create the distinctive stratum pattern, a collection of folded and fractured horizontal lines caused by the slow movement of the earth's crust. A card raked through paint and glaze at differing angles produces a similar, fractured stripe effect.

Stripes

Think of long, thin vertical lines as strict and rigid as soldiers in a row; tall standing grasses wispy and waving in the breeze; broken streaky stripes on a zebra or tiger; long palm fronds; subtly layered strata of rocks; a thicket of bamboo—all comprise different kinds of stripes. They can be in the form of bold bands, thin veins, fluttery streamers, or a few sparse streaks.

Fabric woven on a loom produces stripes naturally. There are wools with simple pinstripes and mattress ticking with fine stripes, as well as kilims and Indian sari fabric with stripes of silver and gold.

Diverse possibilities

Stripes are probably the simplest form of repeated pattern. Their simplicity makes them extremely versatile, so they can take on virtually any style. The repeat can be regular or irregular, and the stripes can be wide or narrow, staggered or even, straight or wobbly, soft- or hard-edged, and horizontal, vertical, or diagonal. The colors of all the stripes can be of similar tone or widely varied, and either plain or patterned.

Whatever their shape and configuration, stripes are enduringly adaptable. Vertical ones are an excellent device for making a low-ceilinged room seem higher. Stripes used horizontally, though more unusual, can give the illusion of extra space to a small area.

Painted stripes can be produced in many different ways, from fine, delicate lines made with a dragging brush to wide, chunky stripes applied with a roller. Graining combs and strips of cardboard can produce strict, straight stripes or loose, fluid lines, while hand-painting gives you more freedom with designs.

"Whether hard- or soft-edged, straight or curvy,
stripes are enduringly adaptable."

Combing

A decorator's comb is similar to a comb used for the hair, that is, a toothed instrument used to pull through and separate something else. In this case, the comb pulls through a layer of colored glaze (see page 121) to create a striped pattern that reveals the base color in places.

Generally, decorators use rubber or plasticized combs, with square, wedge-shaped teeth. A piece of cardboard can also be used, for a less regimented look, as can the fingers–an idea taken from the Ndebele people of southern Africa who traditionally used it to decorate the outsides of their homes. The appeal of the comb lies in its speed, ease of use, and versatility: simple stripes can remain regularly spaced or be made irregular, they can be adapted to make wavy lines or zigzags or be layered in alternate directions to produce checks. For maximum impact, choose strongly contrasting base and glaze colors.

2 Pull the comb down firmly through the glaze, wiping it frequently on a cloth or paper towel to remove the excess glaze that builds up in the teeth. A variety of patterns can be made with the comb; try criss-crossing or making wavy lines. When producing layers of combing in different colors, allow each glaze coat to dry before applying the next.

1 Use a household paintbrush to apply an even, not too thick, layer of colored glaze (see page 121) to the surface. If covering a large area, work in manageable-sized sections, leaving an uncombed edge to work the next area of wet glaze into.

Above: Traditional combs, both with regular and graduated teeth, are relatively small. Larger combs can be made out of cardboard and floor tiles using scissors or a sharp knife.

Using a cardboard comb

Cut or tear a piece of thick cardboard that can be held comfortably in two hands. Apply an even, thin strip of colored glaze to the surface, slightly wider then the card. Position the card at the top of the strip and pull it down firmly and with equal pressure through the glaze. To vary the direction of the stripes pull one hand down more than the other. To make a horizontal line in the glaze, stop moving the card, then change the angle of the card slightly to continue.

Using fingers

Apply colored glaze to a manageable-sized area. Using either two or three fingers, kept the same width apart, pull down through the glaze. Keep the fingers straight or wiggle them to produce different patterns.

Hand-painting stripes

If stripes are to fall vertically down a wall they need to be straight; wavy stripes over such a large expanse will prove disconcerting and unsettling. Hand-painted stripes can look clean and sharp, even though they also have a slightly uneven quality, which makes them comfortable to live with.

A good way to ensure your stripes are straight is to use a length of string with a weight tied at the bottom (a plumb line) as a guideline for your paintbrush. Adhesive putty makes an ideal weight and the makeshift plumb line can be attached to the wall using more adhesive putty. It is also a good idea to use brushes of different widths to fill in wide and thin stripes.

1 Cut several lengths of string the height of the wall. Stick one length of string to the top of the wall using adhesive putty. To keep the string straight as it hangs, wrap adhesive putty around the other end to create a plumb line. Attach several lengths of string and adhesive putty to the wall to make stripes of different widths. Using the string as a guide, fill in the first stripe, using a brush generously loaded with paint. Take your time and remember that as more pressure is applied to the brush the bristles will spread out, making the line wobble.

2 Use the same technique to fill in alternate stripes. You can use different sizes of brush for different widths of stripe, to make the job quicker.

3 Make sure the painted stripes are completely dry before you return to fill in the unpainted ones. Mistakes made with the new paint can be easily wiped away from a dry painted base, but will smudge if wiped away from a wet base.

To paint horizontal stripes, use a spirit level and a large ruler to mark faint pencil lines on the wall, and fill in the stripes as above.

Opposite: One wall of this kitchen is painted with strong, multicolored stripes. The stripes vary in width and depth of color so there is a lot for the eye to look at. Some colors jump out at you, some offer an airy spaciousness, while others are dense and inward. The wall is naturally rough which accentuates the natural wobble in the painted edge and softens the stripes. Cutout paper prints are stuck to the stripes (see page 74) to help emphasize the different tonal qualities in the colors used.

Using rollers

Generally used for applying paint flatly, rollers are also ideal for making stripes. They can be found in several widths and are either long-pile or sponge. The long-pile (or mohair) rollers are fluffy, producing a wobbly, uneven edge, while sponge rollers give a neat, straight edge. The soft edges created with a fluffy roller can be exaggerated by dampening the rollers and working adjacent stripes into the wet edges of the previous strips.

Opposite: Horizontal stripes help give a room a feeling of depth and space, especially when painted in light colors like the blue, lilac, and yellow on this wall. The lightly blurred look is achieved by using sponge rollers in the same way as you would to paint vertical stripes, allowing the colors to overlap and veer slightly to give a soft, informal look.

Left: Choose paint colors that are not too contrastingly different, and prepare them in roller trays before beginning.

3 Continue working in the same way, sometimes letting the roller overlap the previous, still-wet painted stripe to produce different effects and slightly different colors.

1 Prepare some makeshift plumb lines to use as guidelines for alignment (see page 61), or mark horizontal lines on the surface with pencil. Load the first paint color onto a dampened roller and, following your guidelines, roll the paint on in one direction

2 While the paint is still wet, apply another rollerpainted strip in the next color, butting it up to the previous painted stripe.

Left: This single wall called out for a delicate yet rich finish to complement the furniture in the room. I painted a base coat of gold metallic paint (see page 33) and loosely dragged pale plaster pink paint over it. To even up the effect and add some depth, I dragged a layer of gold followed by another dragged coat of plaster pink. The shimmering effect catches the light in places but is not overwhelming.

Dragging

Raw silk, some linen, and other natural fabrics often have a delicate and slightly irregular striped weave. In plant forms, similar fine, lightly striped structures, sometimes only apparent under the microscope, can also be seen. This is nature's finest texture, and an effect that can be simulated with paint using the dragging technique.

When there is little paint on the brush and sweeping movements are made to apply it the result is a series of finely-striped paint marks. A similar finish is achieved if a specialist dragging brush is pulled through colored glaze (see page 121), an effect that gains depth if more than one layer of dragging is applied.

Dragging is particularly effective if the base and glaze coats are close in tone, especially if you are aiming for the look of raw silk. For a stronger look, neutral or metallic colors (see page 33) could be dragged over a very dark, even black base.

Dragging with glaze

1 Paint on the colored glaze (see page 121) in strips. On a wall, start about 1in (2.5cm) below the ceiling and apply a strip of about 18in (45cm) wide to begin with.

2 Take a specialist dragging brush and sweep it up and down the wall, separating the glaze to form loose vertical lines. Do not drag right up to the edge of the strip, but leave an undragged area to work the next strip of glaze into.

3 At the top of a wall, position the dragging brush just below the ceiling. Press down gently on the tip of the bristles and pull the brush down, releasing enough glaze to spread to the ceiling.

Dragging with paint

1 Paint without glaze should be used very dryly–rub excess off on a paper towel– and applied using just the tip of the brush. A large brush is ideal and must not be too densely packed: the bristles should form into points when covered with paint. Applied in this way the paint will form thin, tightly-packed, and uneven stripes that reveal the base color in places.

2 When the first coat is dry, apply a second layer of dragged lines in the same way, using a similarly toned color. This helps to even out any areas of the first coat that were too heavily painted.

More ideas

Stripes are a great solution to any decorating dilemma, whether you want a design that is muted, cool, and formal, or funky and offbeat. Simply combine different paints, techniques, and textures to adapt this foolproof design.

Stripes do not have to be absolutely straight, they can wobble freely and still retain the linear feel, and, whether straight or not, they can also be overlaid to create a range of patterns and effects.

Horizontal lines will add width to a room—perhaps used on just one wall to prevent the effect becoming too overbearing—while vertical stripes can transform a room by adding height. Remember that a stripe does not have to be a solid line of paint, but can be broken up using other techniques such as printing with potato halves to make dotty stripes, or using the frottage technique within the stripes for an overall textured look.

Above: To enliven a simple paneled door, pick out each plank with a stripe of different colored medium-luster paint (see page 21). The luxurious ice cream colors used here combine with the sheen to give a cool, contemporary look.

Opposite top: This wall has been combed to look like rock strata, with flashes of color bursting out in places. First, comb through a layer of gray-blue glaze in straight lines, using a piece of cardboard (see page 59). When this decoration is dry, apply orange and brown glazes in random patches and sometimes mixed together. Comb this layer with cardboard again, using a wobbling motion to produce wavy stripes.

Left: Vivid candy pink stripes stand sentinel along the wall of this study. Work from three separate trays of pinks using only two rollers to apply the paint (see page 62), to ensure that the colors mix. Rather than clean the rollers out, repeatedly reuse the same rollers, allowing the colors to blend naturally together.

Above: Off-white glaze is combed over a blue-black set of drawers using a made-to-measure handmade comb (see page 58), to produce different striped and checked effects. The slightly uneven nature of the stripes and the muted black and white softens what could be a rather hard effect.

"Squares can be quirky and set at odd angles"

Squares & rectangles

Tall, angular pylons punctuating the countryside, and girders forming the skeletons of city buildings, are part of the geometric world we live in now. With technological developments such as reinforced concrete and plate glass and steel structures, geometric design has become the predominant theme in modern decoration. Artists too have taken inspiration from squares and rectangles. Paul Cézanne, and subsequently the cubists, reduced the visual world into cubes, squares, and rectangles, while others, such as Piet Mondrian, used a strict black vertical and horizontal grid with blocks of red, yellow, and white.

Pure geometry

Geometric designs can be mathematically regular, as in a pattern of tiles on a floor, a Japanese paper screen, or a metal lattice grid. A design can have a sharp-edged, steely hardness, with acute angles and a flat texture in positive strong colors. Square black-and-white floor tiles are a classic geometric design, which works in both traditional and contemporary situations. Squares and rectangles do not need to be hard and regimented—they can be quirky and set at odd angles, with soft edges, textured finishes and muted natural colors. Take ideas from patchwork designs or the pattern of fields in the countryside.

Emphasizing the structure

Rooms are basically rectangular, with mainly rectangular pieces of furniture in them. Emphasize the structure by painting oblongs and squares by a window, above a door or along the length of a wall. Paint furniture to bring out the inherent shapes—the doors or drawers can each be treated differently.

Decoration with geometric shapes can take on all sorts of characteristics, from minimal embellishment to complex plaid patterns. Use metallic squares, ready-cut gummed paper squares or a selection of paper shapes you have cut yourself, print squares with a sponge or paint them with rollers and stencils to make geometric design come alive.

Clockwise from top left:
NETWORK
Nets are made to a uniform grid. Rope knitted together to make a network of squares. A web of woven lines that distort and stretch to create a multitude of lozenge and diamond shapes. A grid like this, with straight and wavy lines, can be painted or printed on a wall (see page 78).

DISTORTING REFLECTIONS
Buildings made with plate glass are supported by a distinctive geometric steel structure. The flat windows act like mirrors reflecting other buildings or the sky. Here, shiny convex panels distort reflections of other geometric windows. A metal leaf finish can have a similarly reflective or distorted effect (see page 70).

CIRCLING THE SQUARE
By angling tiles and taking care to change the spaces in between them, mosaics and tile designs can be made to create all manner of rounded shapes, including circles. A circle of squares can be similarly produced using cut paper or stencils (see pages 74 and 77).

TILE STYLE
The arrangement of these stenciled squares (see page 77) was influenced by the idea of tiles, made irregular like mosaics or crazy paving.

Using metal leaf

Modern metals are all around us, from architecture, furniture, and home utensils to technological machinery. To reinvent the qualities of these materials in the home there is nothing to beat metal leaf. No paint can match it for quality of shine.

Aluminum (imitation silver) has a mirror-like whiteness in the light, becoming gray in the shadows. Copper has a deep orange glow and brass (imitation gold) shines a rich yellow in the light. The technique of using metal leaf is not as intimidating as it looks, and the price of materials is affordable, just so long as you do not use too much real gold or silver.

Metal leaf, or foil as it is sometimes called, comes in neat 5 x 5in (12.5 x 12.5cm) squares—real gold and silver leaf squares are usually a little smaller—making it an obvious choice for square patterns. Water-based size (glue) remains tacky indefinitely, so you can either apply size over a large area and add the metal leaf squares, leaving gaps in between as desired, before varnishing to protect the leaf and cover the size, or, alternatively, start by applying a square of size smaller than the leaf and covering the glue completely.

With the exception of aluminum, all leaf tarnishes so it must be varnished to seal it from the air. Any varnish may be used (see page 122).

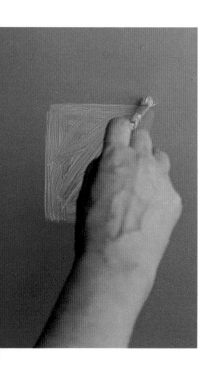

1 Use an old paintbrush to apply a coat of water-based size to the surface. Leave the size for a few minutes until it becomes clear and tacky.

3 Use a very soft brush to smooth the leaf into place and flatten it out. Use a gentle dabbing motion rather than wiping. Any tears or imperfections can be filled with torn pieces of leaf, since the leaf will only adhere to the size in the gap, and the excess around the edges can be wiped away and saved for future repair work. Varnishing the leaf will help flatten it out and remove any roughness.

2 A sheet of metal leaf is extremely light and so at first is difficult to control; you may find the sheet easier to handle if you cover your hands with talcum powder, removing the hands' natural moisture. Try to lay the sheet flat in your hand and then drop one end gently onto the sized surface, gradually letting the whole sheet drop into place.

Opposite: Metal leaf needs strong vibrant colors to show it off to its best advantage. Use small rollers to paint over-lapping, multicolored squares and position individual sheets of aluminum, brass, and copper metal leaf randomly over the effect, like a modern, glistening patchwork quilt.

Glazing checks

The basis of any checked design is that horizontal and vertical lines cross, and when it comes to fabrics, the intersection of woven lines also creates a third color: think of brightly colored Madras cotton sarongs, silken sari material with silver and gold threads, simple gingham, and complex tartans with heather tones.

To produce painted checked designs, simply create a grid using rollers of varying widths and space the components at different distances. The grid can be regular or irregular, the gaps in between can be large or small, but consider using only two or three colors to begin with, to keep the design simple and not too overbearing. Using translucent colored glaze (see page 121) is what gives a painted checked pattern that "fabric" feel, because when you overlap colors you create new shades.

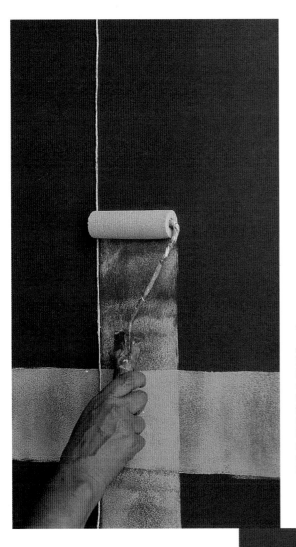

1 First mix two or three colored glazes (see page 121). Hang a makeshift plumb line from the top of the wall (see page 61). Load a sponge roller with the first glaze mixture and lightly apply to the wall (see page 115), following the plumb line. To keep a horizontal stripe straight, make marks on the wall in pencil, using a spirit level for accuracy.

2 Cut another sponge roller with a sharp pair of scissors to make it narrow.

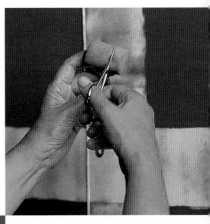

Opposite: Complementing the grid-based structure of the shelving unit, this wall is painted with a checked design inspired by fabrics from Asia. The original rich blue wall would have contrasted strongly with the silver paint I intended to use, so to soften the base, I applied a pale turquoise colorwash (see page 108). I then rollerpainted on silver metallic paint (see page 33) mixed with glaze, and added hand-painted lines in turquoise matte paint (see page 14).

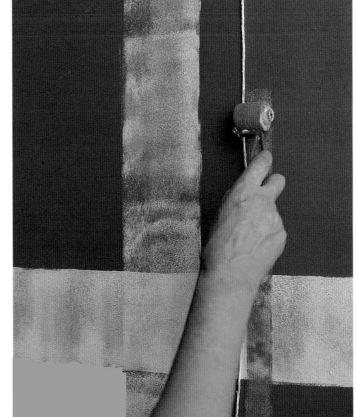

3 Reposition the plumb line and roll on the second color using the cut roller, overlapping the horizontal line. Alternate between wide and narrow rollers and between overlaps—sometimes the horizontal will overlap the vertical—building up a checked pattern. To complete the look, use a fine artist's brush to hand paint thin lines of slightly diluted paint (see page 96) on top of, or adjacent to, the rollerpainted stripes.

Paper squares

Using geometric cut paper brings together two ideas from modern art: the use of flat, abstract compositions of squares and rectangles explored by the Dutch artist Mondrian, and the use of cutouts in colored paper seen in the work of the French artist, Henri Matisse.

Adapting these ideas to your own specifications opens up a range of possibilities. You can cut geometric shapes accurately, or let them stray a little from the rigid, 90-degree-angles rule, or mix the two: squares and rectangles of different sizes, some irregularly cut and some very neat could look stunning. You may choose to apply the shapes regularly, like a grid, or in a seemingly random way, allowing the shapes to "float" in space. However, do bear in mind that this technique can be difficult and tiring if carried out across a large wall. Remember also that there is no need to cover a wall, a few strategically placed pieces is often enough, and consider the importance of the space around the shapes as well as the shapes themselves.

Use plain paper, foreign newspapers in exotic scripts, comics, or magazine covers to produce a variety of different styles. Remember that paper intended for ephemeral use is not designed to last; newspaper is likely to discolor and tissue papers fade in the sun.

1 Cut out your squares or rectangles, of equal size, as here, or in varying sizes. Apply glue to the surface in the area needed. Any glue can be used but it is recommended that wallpaper paste be used as this enables the paper to be removed easily at a later date.

2 Position one side of the paper first and then gently smooth the rest of the shape into place by wiping it with a damp sponge. Continue working over the paper with the sponge to remove air bubbles and trapped glue, ensuring no creases remain. Wipe away excess glue and dye from the paper with a freshly dampened sponge and continue applying more squares or rectangles in the pattern of your choice.

Opposite: With just three different colored papers, two browns and a gray, an arrangement of squares of different sizes adorns one wall in this modern apartment. Here the shapes are placed with a similar distance between them but, for added tension, the cut paper can be positioned at dramatically discordant angles and spaced irregularly.

Geometric stenciling

Opposite: The walls in the kitchen area of this very modern warehouse apartment are stenciled in coffee, ice blue, and biscuit colors on a chocolate-colored background. Starting on a dark background helps to give your design "body" and gives maximum impact to a simple repeating motif. Here, I used four uneven square stencils to make up this simple decoration, including a few smaller ones overprinted to give a little depth.

The essence of modern abstract geometric work is the flatness of the shapes. To recreate this look in the home, stenciling with a roller is the ideal technique.

An abstract design must have balance, yet without regimental repetition or anything too predictable. Just such a design can be assembled easily by cutting shapes from any thin card—cereal packets for example, or specialist stencil card—and arranging them to give a mechanical look. Using a brush to stencil results in visible brushstrokes, but a small roller quickly produces the distinctive "flat" look.

The secret of success behind any stenciling work is to use a very small amount of paint and to ensure that the paint is not too watery: thick amounts of paint will run under the stencil and become otherwise very difficult to control.

2 Position the stencil and hold it in place with your hand, or use masking tape or a spray repositioning glue. Load a small roller with a little paint, wiping away excess on a sheet of paper towel. Roll the paint repeatedly over the stencil to produce a solid but slightly uneven texture.

1 Using a sharp craft knife, cut squares and rectangles from a sheet of thin but firm card. Do this with or without the guidance of a ruler and do not make the shapes too regular: angle the sides to make quirky alternatives.

3 Roller the paint around the edge of the card to make an 'L' shape.

Making a grid

Instead of making solid squares and rectangles, the same shapes can be indicated by making lines. As with grids, netting, graph paper, or lattice, the geometric shapes are formed in the spaces between the lines, resulting in a lighter and less dense effect.

A grid can be painted regularly and accurately or, for an offbeat feel, the lines can be wobbly and positioned at slightly different angles to create irregular shapes. For sharp, crisp lines, use masking tape to paint a grid, but for a quicker and less rigid finish you can print lines with cardboard.

Opposite: This design, using a grid shape, is colored irregularly with rectangles of solid paint. The pattern is reminiscent of designs for kitchen crockery from the 1950s, when the cell shape became prevalent in all aspects of design, and the light, bright colors give the dining area of this kitchen an airy feel.

3 Cardboard from packing boxes provides a firm but absorbent surface to print with. Apply some paint to the edge of the cardboard with a brush. The paint must not be too thin and runny, or too thick and blobby. Test a little before working on the finished surface.

4 Press the edge of the cardboard onto the surface using even pressure. It may be possible to get two prints from each application of paint but, if the second print looks a little weak, apply new paint after every print.

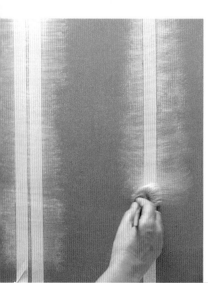

1 Choose a low-tack masking tape of the desired width. The tape will mask out the paint and produce a "negative" strip when it is removed. Position strips of low-tack masking tape on the surface, making sure the tape is well adhered to prevent paint seeping underneath. Apply the paint with a dry brush using very little paint. Slowly build up the solidity of color.

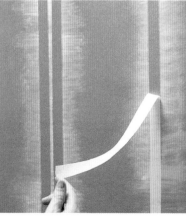

2 Remove the tape as soon as the paint has been applied; do not wait for it to dry.

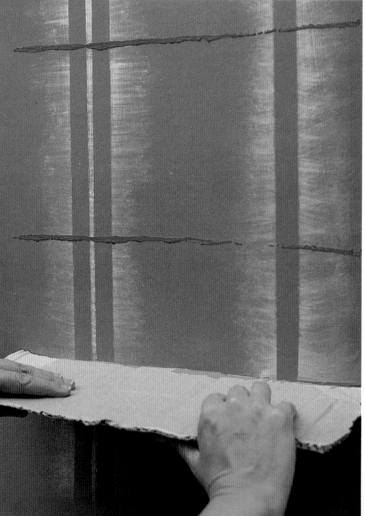

More ideas

Geometric designs are especially effective and easy to reproduce on flat surfaces or on box-like pieces of furniture such as a chest of drawers or bedside cabinet: the style emphasizes the solid, three-dimensional feel of an object. Remember, however, that the squares or rectangles themselves do not have to be perfectly straight, or mathematically correct.

Print, paint, or stencil with any of the paints featured in this book—shiny finishes like pearlized or metallic paint look great—or fill in the squares with a textured effect; frottaged squares of color on a floor look like large slabs of stone. Alternatively, do not be afraid to combine geometrics with stripes or spots.

Left: Recreate a variation on black-and-white tiles on a wall by simply printing matte black paint (see page 14) over a white base using a square sponge (see page 85). Use a piece of weighted string to help keep the verticals straight (see page 61).

Left: Use purple, blue and red glazes to paint a rough-edged checked pattern (see page 73) on a small cabinet. Glue manuscript paper featuring a free flowing, cursive typeface into the center of the cabinet (see page 74) to contrast with the check.

Right: Gild squares of aluminium leaf (see page 70) over a very dark blue-gray base, emphasizing the square shapes by leaving gaps in between each sheet. To soften the effect, rub away the leaf a little in places using a little water and coarse steel wool. Varnish to seal.

Right: This 1950s style table is decorated with a design based on overlapping squares and rectangles inspired by fabric designs. Randomly stencil geometric shapes of varying sizes in neutrals like gray and beige, offset by dark red, pink and two shades of green. For a high sheen finish, varnish the surface with a gloss varnish (see page 122).

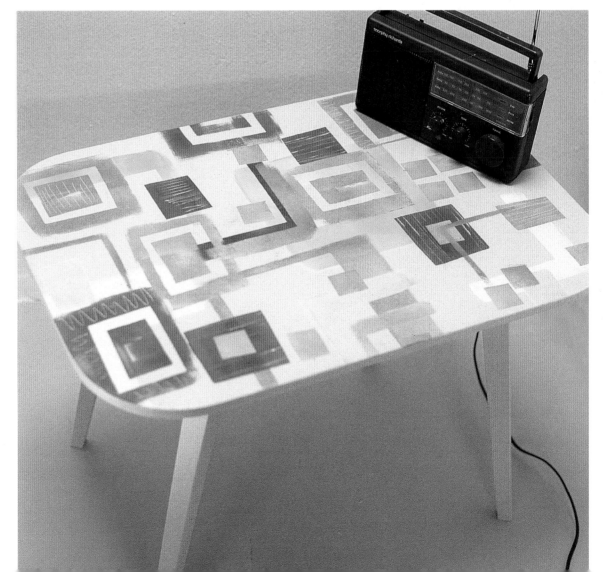

Spots, dots, & circles

Clockwise from top left:
CIRCLES IN CIRCLES
Spherical lime fruits in a round basket make an arrangement of overlapping circles. The lemon spots interspersed in the lime colors, along with the sunlight and shadows, create a tight and complex dotty arrangement that can be simulated with bright paints.

SUMMER SPOTS
I used a patterned roller (see page 90) to reproduce the look of brightly colored flowers in a summer meadow. Some dots overlap, others sit perfectly while some smudge, the light flower colors contrasting with the rich green.

DAISY DOTS
A collection of daisies, the flower heads looking in the same direction, searching for the sun, grows in clusters. Some of the flowers overlap, others are isolated against an irregularly mottled green. Reverse stencil overlapping circular shapes to create the same clustered, natural feel (see page 86).

CELL STRUCTURE
These spots are virus particles, stained for greater visibility. Appearing in seemingly rambling rows, the ringed cells form an irregular honeycomb arrangement. Glossy translucent paints, used freehand or printed, can make a similar pattern (see pages 26 and 77).

Through space missions sending awe-inspiring pictures of our galaxy back to earth, and powerful microscopes looking more deeply into the structures of our everyday life, we have been able to see previously hidden worlds. Now we perceive our universe as being made up of spots, dots, and circles, from tiny atoms to enormous stars. These are the constantly recurring shapes in both the microcosm of the microscopic world and the macrocosm of the universe.

As a result, a huge new area of abstract ideas has opened up for both artists and designers. The French painter Georges Seurat was one of the first to break pictures up into dots, in his pointillist paintings. Later, the Spanish artist Joán Miró painted semi-abstracts featuring amoeba-like circles with dots, stars, and moons.

From microscope to telescope

Under the microscope, all manner of circular molecular structures can be seen. Some are sharply defined, others have a wavy outline, while still others are fuzzy or have a double edge. The visual images from space have been increasingly inspiring, as we discover the colors and textures of supernovas, nebulas, and asteroids.

Dots are everywhere. The printed page when enlarged reveals that pictures in books, magazines, and newspapers are made up of lots of dots. Spots appear in sunlight dappled by trees, splodged markings on a leopard's back, oval pebbles on a beach. They can be the holes in a pegboard or the dots in polka-dot fabric or in the Dreamtime paintings of Australian Aborigines. Whether regular or random, they offer the modern painter and decorator a shape that can be the basis of decoration that is either formal or informal, minimal or bohemian and executed using everything from a plasterer's roller to a plastic cup.

"Spots, dots and circles are the constantly recurring shapes of the universe"

Left: Like a summer garden full of flowers, this table sings with color. First, paint the table with random patches of dark and strong colors, including black. Then print solid and hollow circles, spots, and dots of all sizes in lighter and brighter colors using a large plastic bowl, sheets of bubble wrap in different sizes, the base of a plastic cup, a continental paintbrush, the end of a sponge roller, and a wine cork. Some larger circles can be overprinted with smaller spots to look like flowers, while other prints can be left abstract.

Stamping

Producing printed impressions by applying paint to the flat surface of a household object and pressing it onto a surface is a very direct and easy way to make designs. Choose a variety of items that are circular, such as corks, plastic cups or bowls, a sheet of bubble wrap, and the end of a sponge roller, and keep handy a selection that will produce circles and spots of different sizes and textures.

Try to keep the colors used for the stamping and the background similarly toned, to be sure of a pleasing effect that is not too jarring. Alternatively, work with a dark background and apply strong, bright, light colors for a dramatic contrast. To avoid a raised print, apply small amounts of paint to the stamps each time.

Collect a selection of objects that can be used to stamp impressions of spots and circles of varying sizes. Dilute thick paint with water and test the prints on some spare paper first: the paint must not be too thick and splodgy or too runny, but of a consistency that makes an even print. Apply a little paint to the surface of the object using a brush or roller and press the object firmly and with even pressure, onto the surface. Reapply paint to the stamp after one or two uses. Here, we have used the cut-off end of a sponge roller, a hollow garden cane, the rim of a plastic cup, a wine cork, a continental paintbrush, and some torn corrugated cardboard bent into a circular shape.

Reverse stenciling

The repertoire of the modern painter and decorator is constantly growing, and ideas come from many other disciplines. For example, some methods of fabric printing with silk screens work on the principle of blocking the ink from parts of a design, a simple idea that is easily translated to paint and requires little in the way of equipment. A reverse stencil is a solid shape cut from card that blocks out paint. Take the card stencil away and the shape is depicted in the base color.

Circles of various sizes are easy to cut and can be combined to look like many different shapes. Cut out lots of templates if a large area is to be painted since, if it is repeatedly used, a card stencil will soon become saturated and unusable.

1 Collect together a selection of round objects which can be drawn around. Draw the templates onto some thin but firm card or specialist stencil card, and cut out the shapes.

Opposite: A simple wooden candlestick is given an individual and quirky look using reinforcement stickers for ring binders. Reverse stenciled in several layers, using thick brushstrokes of matte paint (see page 14) in orange and blue, the result is a random arrangement of dots and spots. When dry, rub the candlestick lightly with a damp cloth to take off part of the top layer of paint and produce a textured look.

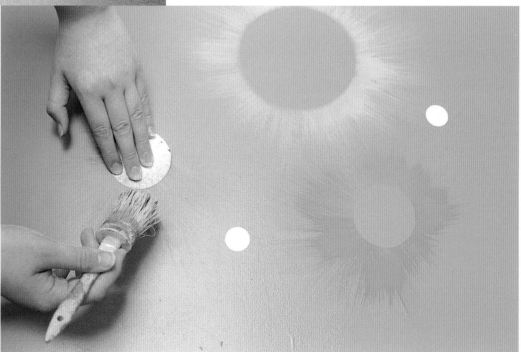

2 Hold the card in position and use a brush to paint around it, radiating out from the center. When the stencil is removed the remaining design—a "negative" circle with paint all around it—looks like a sun or flower shape. Repeat the idea with large and small spots to build up a pattern.

Spotted stone

Opposite: The floor in this apartment has a natural stone look produced using colors in keeping with the aluminum finish of the windows. Over a very deep blue-green base, lay a soft off-white glaze and spatter with water alone. Then flick on tiny amounts of diluted terracotta-red paint to give depth and life to the finish.

Many beautiful floors are formed from natural materials like polished stone and marble that give sleek surfaces. Alternatively, man-made materials such as linoleum and terrazzo are easier to locate and lay, making them popular in apartment blocks and industrial buildings, where strong flooring is necessary. Both materials carry a spotted, varied design that looks like natural stone.

A natural stone finish can be reproduced using a paint and glaze mixture (see page 121), water, and a sponge roller. This technique can only be carried out on a flat surface, and a floor should be tackled in small areas of about 6ft (2m) square. It is also important to varnish the finish (see page 122) several times to provide a practical, hard-wearing surface.

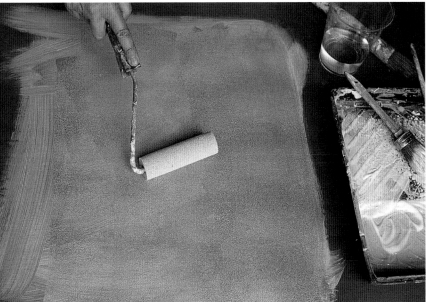

1 Mix a translucent colored glaze (see page 121). Apply the mixture to a manageable-sized area using a paintbrush (above). Go over the glazed square with a sponge roller to soften the brushmarks, leaving a smooth, even surface (right).

3 Run the roller lightly over the still-wet surface to absorb the water flicks, revealing the base color underneath. To add extra color, dilute a very small amount of paint in some water and flick this onto the glazed surface, but do not go over the effect with the roller.

2 Using a small, hard-bristled paintbrush, spray or lightly flick water onto the glazed surface. At first it will be invisible, but the effect will soon become more apparent.

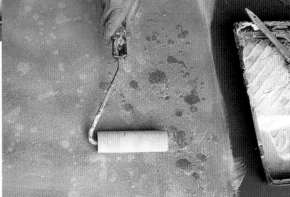

Using patterned rollers

A build-up of tiny dots, like a section of an impressionist painting, can be painted using a special roller covered with small raised nodules that is normally used to apply textured plaster effects.

The look is similar to the work of Georges Seurat, the French painter who, in the 1880s, devised a painting technique known as pointillism, whereby small dots of pure and complementary color covered the canvas. When seen from afar the dots merge and the work is of startling brilliance. To achieve that same depth and luminosity, several layers of paint can be applied, and the effect looks particularly good when a light color is applied over a deep or bright color.

Opposite: Layers of bright blue, pink, and lemon yellow are lightly rolled over a rich leafy green base on this wall. Allow each layer to dry before applying the next color in random directions, grouping together predominantly pink and yellow in some places and blue and yellow in others. The eye sees new colors emerging where the layers overlap and the effect is subtle yet lively, providing a fresh contrast to the adjacent cement-rendered wall.

1 Pour a small amount of paint into the roller tray and pull the roller through it so that just the tips are covered.

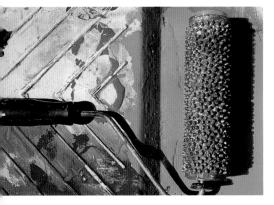

2 It is a good idea to test the movement of the roller on some spare paper before committing to your surface. Roll the paint over the surface to make a spotty effect. The roller should be repeatedly applied to the surface, always with just a little paint on it each time, to make a myriad of tiny spots.

3 When the first covering of paint is dry, repeat the process with a second, similarly toned color. Drips may occur and should be wiped away immediately.

More ideas

Spots, more than any other motif, have a reputation as an unsophisticated pattern: polka dots in primary colors are what usually springs to mind. But work them in chic colors with stylish finishes and they can look elegant and refined.

Spots can have sharp or woolly edges, they can be mechanical or soft and they can be combined with any other pattern, including the geometric stripes and squares. Paint, print, or stencil spots against a textured background–such as a frottaged finish–and they will be enlivened with depth and richness.

Below: Inspired by flower-power fabric from the 1960s, a spattering of reverse-stenciled spots (see page 86), like flowers and suns, covers these walls. Apply mustard yellow, olive green, and cream paints over card circles of various sizes onto a lilac base. Working with a random overall design like this one allows scope for experimentation; in places, stencil the shapes in isolation, while in other areas overprint paints to produce clusters of motifs.

Left: I used a potato cut in half (see page 85) to randomly stamp ovals in chocolate brown and purple-blue across this kitchen wall. The biscuit-brown base color warms the blue and softens the brown. This method of stamping will always give a surface great variety, since the texture of each print will be different. Try to use as little paint as possible to avoid producing a lumpy, heavy and raised print.

Above: To produce woolly–looking spots like these, use a large, round-ended bristly brush and a little paint (see page 85). Stamp the paint on in two colors, randomly positioning the dots. The background was lightly rollerpainted on (see page 115) in a parchment shade and mud brown over gray.

Right: A look similar to that of a guinea fowl's plumage is reproduced on this black stool, by dabbing white paint all over with a small, soft-haired brush (see page 85). The soft bristles rarely produce perfectly round shapes, but spontaneous dashes or oval shapes give the piece a playful feel.

Offbeat designs

Modern designs have an offbeat, off-center look. The quirky and the irregular are admired more than the traditional look, in which designs tend to have an altar-like symmetry or adhere to classical rules of proportion. In modern design it is the exception rather than the rule that is sought, creating not order but random, illogical, and incidental arrangements. This seeming chaos can, paradoxically, produce an odd sense of balance and a creative, dynamic tension.

Arresting images

Through photography in television, films, and advertisements, we have become accustomed to odd viewpoints, angles, and close-ups. Our eyes are now accustomed to the collage effect of different images superimposed on each other. Like peering through a microscope, close-ups of seemingly unimportant details become fascinating in their own right and take on a life of their own. Images are half-seen, and a single brushstroke turns into an abstract design. Calligraphy is appreciated as it does not involve the distraction of having to read the words.

Asymmetrical patterns

A modern asymmetrical design can be created in several ways. It can be randomly applied, like dribbled paint that makes no detectable pattern, or the incidental flick and swipe of the brush; or it may consist of doodles done idly in wet paint. Images can be distorted, like turning paving-slab shapes into crazy paving. Disparate images from magazines can be torn out and arranged together in themes.

Clockwise from top left:

'NUMBER 6, 1948'
This painting by American artist Jackson Pollock (1912–1956) uses paint poured in speedy loops and trails along with slower dribbles. Dribble paint over a frottaged floor to produce the same depth without the manic intensity (see pages 26, 99 and 112).

STUDIO FLOOR
Over the years, an offbeat pattern has built up in places on this studio floor, from dribbles and spills of multicolored paints. The serendipitous design has been reinvented across the whole floor by dribbling, flicking, and pouring paint in many layers (see page 99).

AMERICAN GRAFFITI
Stylized lettering distorts words and personal signatures. The marks are overlaid so that just a few letters can be made out, while everything else turns into an abstract, offbeat arrangement. Overlay thick brushmarks to create a seemingly fluid pattern (see page 96).

CAUGHT IN TIME
Colored beams of light are moved in squiggles and loops by an unseen hand. Caught by a long camera exposure, the lines are unvaried in width but make a random pattern set against a dark background. Incise through paint with the same freedom and fluidity to create unique patterns (see page 100).

"In modern design, the chaotic and the unexpected are sought"

Brushwork

One of the hallmarks of modern art is the importance of the brushmark. In traditional painting, the brushwork was hidden as artists concentrated on making a painting look real, not like a painting. However, in the 19th century the brushstroke became a vital part of the artist's vocabulary, when the mechanics of the work were considered as important as the scene depicted. The Swiss painter Paul Klee described his work as "taking the line for a walk," illustrating the trend of exploring all aspects and expressions of the line.

Brushmarks can be thick, thin, fat, or scratchy. A painted line can be slow and deliberate or fast and indefinite. The mark you want to make will be defined by the brush you use. Brushes are made from either firm bristles or soft, fine hair and they come in a variety of shapes and sizes. Bristle brushes produce the wild and expressive lines of modern paint effects and individual brush lines are especially apparent if only a little paint is used. A smoother, clearer and more defined brushmark will be created using a natural hair brush.

Practice will help you find the necessary light and varied touch with the brushes and will also furnish you with some interesting brushmarks.

Dots

Use a round-ferruled brush, either with round or pointed bristles, to make spots. Load the brush with paint in the same way as before, then dot the tips of the bristles onto the surface. Use more pressure on the bristles to produce a looser, less defined round shape.

Thick straight line

Take a large brush. Dip the bristles in the paint until just over half the brush is immersed, then press the bristles against the side of the container to remove the excess paint. Repeat until the bristles are sufficiently and evenly covered: there should be enough paint on the brush to complete a whole line without paint dripping when the brush is pressed on the surface.

To make a straight vertical or horizontal line, apply the paint by moving the upper arm, not the wrist: the arm muscles may get tired and can be supported with the other hand. Some people find that taking a firm hold of the brush at the ferrule is easier and more controllable than holding the handle.

Concentrate your vision on a point just ahead of the brush, rather than on the painted line itself.

Fluid line

Take a chisel-shaped brush—this one is flat but you can also use a chisel-shaped brush with a slight point. Fill the brush as suggested above, then think of the brush as a calligraphic pen. Hold it in a diagonal position to start with and pull down. To make the line widen, turn the brush until the chisel end is horizontal and exert a little more pressure. Turn back to make the line thinner again.

Geometrics

Use either a square or chisel-shaped brush to paint squares and rectangles. Here, a firm, soft-haired brush was used to produce neat and fairly precise shapes with clean edges. Load the brush with paint as before. Position the tip of the brush on the surface at an angle of 45 degrees and pull down. Cleanly lift off the brush when the desired shape is complete.

Below: Fat and fine brushstrokes streak across this wall making dynamic and powerful shapes. Some of the lines are broken and others are continuous but in no particular order. Use paints with a reflective quality, medium-luster, metallic gold, and pearlized (see pages 20–21, 32–33 and 38–39), over a black glossy translucent base (see pages 26–27), for maximum impact.

Dribbling paint

Dribbling paint–allowing it to fall from a brush held a little above the surface–is part of the modern paint vocabulary and a technique inspired by Jackson Pollock, the American artist who, in the late 1940s and 1950s, made an art form out of dribbling and spattering paint in many layers.

Dribbling paint onto a surface looks easy, but to get any measure of control it is essential that the paint is of exactly the right consistency. Too wet and the result is puddles of paint, too dry and the paint refuses to run off the brush.

Needless to say, this technique can only be carried out on a horizontal surface, so for furniture and floors it is ideal. It is also easier to use just one or two colors–a few light or bright colors over a deeper base for example–than attempting many colors as Pollock did.

Opposite: I wanted this floor to be a strong focus of attention without being too busy. To produce the necessary depth, I first frottaged the floor in similarly toned shades of blue and brown (see page 112). I then dribbled and flicked white and black glossy translucent paints (see page 26), thinking carefully about the direction of movement.

1 Mix any water-based paint with some water and test the consistency by pressing a full brush on the rim of the container. The paint should roll down the side of the container slowly but surely.

2 Load an artist's brush with diluted paint and hold it over the surface. Allow the paint to flow off the brush while drawing in the air, gently flicking at random intervals to produce a dynamic line.

Incising

While traditional painters applied paint to the surface, modern artists and designers have also experimented with removing paint. Wet paint is worked into with a thin implement, as if drawing, to reveal the color beneath, a technique that allows the artist a lot of freedom; mistakes can easily be painted over.

A free and loose design, like doodles and scribbles, works well with this technique and inspiration can be found in the work of the Spanish artist Joán Miró who used black lines against scarlet, yellow, and azure blue. The loops and circles used repeatedly in handwriting practice guides can also spark ideas.

1 Apply the base coat, which will be revealed by the incised design, and leave to dry. Here, we have randomly applied several colors to provide an interesting background. Mix the top coat paint with a little glaze (see page 121), enough to prevent it drying too quickly, but not so much that the mixture becomes translucent. Use a brush to apply the top coat.

2 Using the end of a thin paintbrush for fine lines, or an eraser for thicker lines, draw freehand loops, circles, spikes and loose lines into the wet glaze, revealing the color beneath.

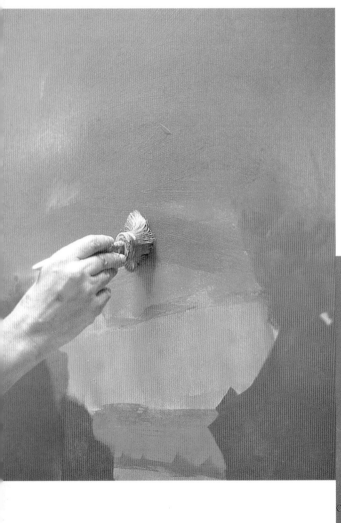

Opposite: Lines of loops work their way across the walls of this dining room, disclosing patches of red, white, and yellow. Over the red walls I applied patches of white and yellow paint mixed with a little glaze and used an eraser to incise the wet paint with lines of loops. To create more depth, I then applied a layer of gray paint and glaze in patches over the previous dry decoration, and incised it in the same way.

Collage

When you are building up a collage effect using abstract or representational images from good-quality magazines, it is a good idea to work with a theme, rather than a random selection of pictures. Here a collection of images on the theme of stripes has been gathered. Your selection can include a variety of "types" of image, from architectural plans to ancient art, using human forms or natural themes to industrial and engineering models. Once you are happy with your collection, take some time positioning the images to find an arrangement that shows them to their best advantage.

Opposite: To create a strong visual effect in a minimally designed kitchen, a collage is worked on just part of one wall. The theme of faces, following a color scheme based around browns and grays, is worked in three stripes of different widths, with a contrasting stripe built up from natural images with a green and brown color scheme. Tear pictures from magazines and stick them down, overlapping slightly over a deep blue background.

Tearing

Tearing the paper is a softer and less laborious method than cutting pictures out with a pair of scissors. Decide whether you want white edges around your images. Take the paper in both hands. Pull the the right hand towards you, then pull the left hand towards you. One of the directions pulled will reveal the white tearmark in the paper. Keep the fingers fairly close to the tearing to keep control of the picture.

Arrangements

The pictures you have chosen can be arranged in lines, squares, or panels as well as covering a whole wall. When you have decided on an arrangement, apply glue to the surface in the desired position. Any glue can be used but wallpaper paste is the best choice if you need to remove the collage at a later date. Lay the torn paper in place and smooth over it with a damp sponge. If you do not plan on taking the collage down, varnish it (see page 122) to prevent colors fading.

Above: When dribbling paint (see page 99) on a box, tackle each side separately, allowing the paint on one side to dry before starting on the next. Here, I used cream paint to dribble over a chocolate brown base: the colors are contrasting, yet soft.

Right: I mentally divided this wall into a grid pattern and filled in each of the rectangles with a shape. I used various brushmarks (see page 96), incised squiggles (see page 100) and handprints all along the wall to show some variety, while at the same time balancing the shapes, colors, and motif weights, so that the wall is never too heavy or too light in any one area.

More ideas

Since offbeat techniques, particularly dribbling paint and brushwork, can become too wild and unstructured, I find that it can be useful to work within a grid or to make stripes to give the design some shape. Collage, geometric motifs, or spots on a dribbled background can give a firmer definition to an otherwise potentially rather shapeless design.

You cannot practice offbeat designs, and often they will materialize themselves, sometimes out of completely different techniques. Yet you can control the depth and finish of the offbeat look by carefully choosing the paint to use.

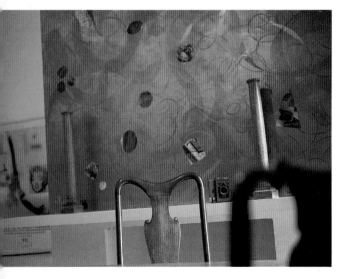

Left: To give the wall over this mantelpiece a rich and lustrous look, I applied gold metallic paint mixed with a little glaze (see pages 33 and 121) over a purple base and incised into it with a small eraser (see page 100). I used a fine comb in places to make regular stripes (see page 58) which break up the pattern. Finally, I tore circles from magazines, concentrating on toning browns and grays, and stuck them on in clusters and in isolation (see page 108).

Opposite: The black, inverted newsprint on this wall has an offbeat, casual look that is unimposing yet has a strong presence. Over a yellow medium-luster base (see page 21), frottage a light gray glaze (see page 112), leaving some sheets of newspaper in position for longer than usual, to allow the print to transfer to the surface.

Patination

RUSTY GLAMOR
The chrome and the black paint on this once shiny, flashy car has faded, dulled, rusted, and discolored. The colors and textures inspire the use of metallic and matte paints in combination, either stippled or frottaged (see pages 33, 14, 111 and 112).

CRACKED EARTH
The land in times of drought, parched and opened up in fissures and cracks, has become a familiar sight. Use mud and clay colors with a crackle varnish to create a similar pattern of irregular shapes (see page 116).

SUBTLE TEXTURE, BOLD COLOR
Natural textures like sandstone, granite, and slate contain a mixture of colors that almost merge into each other. This subtle two-tone effect can be replicated with any of the patination techniques. Use the frottage technique in biscuit colors or, as here, experiment with a bolder color choice (see page 112).

LICHEN ON A ROCK WALL
A rock coated with lichens and moss has indeterminate patches and speckles. Here, muted green with a bright seaweed green mingles with grays, both dark and light, as well as browns. Use the same natural colors for a frottage, perhaps over a stippled base, to achieve a similar depth and texture (see pages 112 and 111).

The mellow look and feel of a surface–its patina–develops over years of exposure to wind, water, temperature extremes, wear-and-tear, and dirt. Whether the material is natural or manmade, the process of patination produces beautifully subtle, sparse, undefined textural patterns. The patina on, say, the bark of a tree, lichen on roof tiles, or the green film on a bronze statue is an intricate organic assemblage. In the landscape, an infinite variety of patinas occur–for example, different types of pebbles and rocks, formed over eons, have textures ranging from smooth and subtle to scratchy and strong. Man-made surfaces, such as rusting metals, wood from which the paint is peeling, and weathered granular concrete buildings, can also have a wonderful patina.

Textures, especially those created by patination, define and lend character to colors and are as important as the colors themselves. Texture seems to add another dimension as you look deep into a surface, rather like looking into the depths of a pond.

Texture and minimalism

Textures are particularly important in minimal styles of interior decoration, where the design is pared down as much as possible. Minimalism, which often utilizes industrial materials, can look too impersonal and bland without a variety of textures. By the same token, a room decorated even in just one color can be made interesting and sophisticated through the skilled use of textural effects.

The subtleness of the painted effect is achieved mainly by using similarly toned colors. Colorwashing, frottaging, and rollerpainted effects give an uneven look while stipple has a neater, more contained appearance.

"Textures lend character to colors, adding another dimension"

Colorwashing

Modern abstract artists have shown how to use paint to its greatest advantage by applying it with variety and vigor, making texture an all important factor: in places paint may be thick and opaque, while in other areas it is thin and almost clear. In the same way, texture and an impression of movement made from wide sweeps of flowing brushwork is what colorwashing is all about.

There are two ways of colorwashing. The first is to apply a colored glaze (see page 121) to a surface, then wipe it off lightly with a cloth making uneven strokes of color through which the base color can be seen. Alternatively, you can apply the colored glaze directly to the surface in criss-cross motions using a large brush. Both methods produce the effect of an uneven wash of color which can either be dynamic and active or quiet and mysterious, depending on the colors chosen and the translucence of the glaze mixture.

1 Combine glaze and paint to reach the desired strength of color (see page 121). The more glaze used the slower the mixture will dry and the color will be more translucent. Apply in an uneven manner with a large brush to an area roughly 3ft (1m) square.

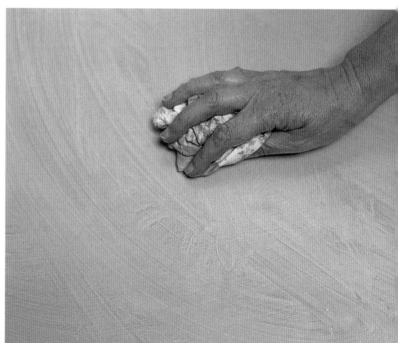

2 Leave the glaze for a few minutes to dry a little. Before it has dried completely, wipe the glazed area with a soft cloth working in every direction with both long and short strokes, and varying degrees of pressure. Use linear or circular strokes. Leave an uncolorwashed border around the edge of the glazed area and when you apply the next, adjacent, patch of glaze, work back into the wet edge. When the first colorwash is completely dry you can repeat the technique with a similarly toned color.

Opposite: Tropical colors, hot and rich, give this sun-filled conservatory an exotic look. I colorwashed a sharp pink and an acid turquoise-blue, in succession, over a previous, earthy, terracotta colorwash.

Stippling

Stippling is a great technique for making hard or strong modern colors a little softer and easier to live with, while neutral colors in a cooler, more minimal look, can feel bland without textural interest, a problem that stippling with two similarly toned shades will discreetly remedy.

A specialist stippling brush, or any brush with a flat surface of short, rigid bristles, is dabbed firmly into a coat of wet glaze (see page 121) to reveal the base color in a series of tiny speckles that can only be seen on close inspection.

Be inspired by the colors of rust, stone, and sand and you will be able to see how the technique can be used to imitate the texture of rocks like sandstone, or rusted and pitted metals that have a beautiful variegated texture with delicate flecks of color.

Opposite: In this kitchen, the design and colors are kept simple, echoing the stainless steel of the taps and sinks. Mix silver metallic paint with glaze and make a rough stipple effect using the brush from a dustpan set. The subtle effect gives a slight texture without dominating as an obvious pattern.

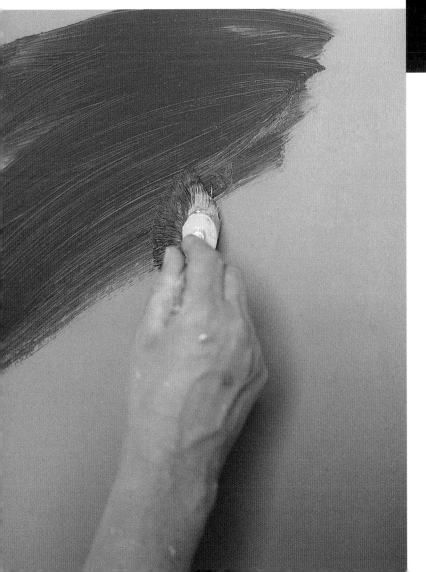

1 Paint on a colored glaze (see page 121) to an area of about 3ft (1m) square, brushing it out in all directions.

2 Use the flat of a specialist stippling brush (top), or, for a wilder, more pronounced pattern, an old bristle hand brush (above), to firmly tap the wet glaze, distributing it over a wider area and revealing the base color in tiny dots. Leave a border of unstippled glaze all around. Apply the next section of glaze, working back into the unstippled wet edge of the previous glaze patch, and continue as before.

When the first stipple is completely dry, you may want to repeat the technique with a similarly toned color.

Frottage

Frottage means "to rub", and this technique is based on a method used by the German surrealist artist Max Ernst, who laid paper over a textured surface and rubbed it with crayon, producing a random, automatic image that he used in his work. Here, the technique is altered slightly, so that it is the paper itself that creates the random, textured effect.

Over a dry base color, a paint and glaze mixture (see page 121) is applied, then newspaper is used to make a textured impression, revealing the base color in places. The newspaper can be used flat and smooth, leaving a thin line where the fold of the paper has been, or it can be crumpled to give a more broken-up effect. Make sure you are prepared when frottaging a complete room: you will need plenty of newspaper at the ready and rubbish bags to collect the used sheets, ensuring you do not end up ankle deep in paper.

For best results use a matte paint for the top coat (see pages 12–15); a satin latex paint may cause the newspaper print to rub off on the surface.

Opposite: Two clay colors, gray and fawn brown, frottaged one over the other, give this staircase wall a look reminiscent of textured concrete. The natural colors are similarly toned so they work wonderfully well together for a subtle effect.

1 Apply colored glaze (see page 121) to an area slightly larger than a sheet of newspaper. Brush the glaze out so that it is not too thick, but do not spread it out too far where it will have time to dry and become unworkable before the next sheet of paper is applied.

2 Lay an open sheet of newspaper on the glazed panel and smooth your hands all over it, ensuring good contact is made all over. Remove the paper immediately. Apply another panel of glaze as before, working back into the previous area of glaze not covered by newspaper. Repeat the process with a fresh sheet of newspaper.

Left: Several shades of blue and green were lightly rollerpainted over this wall, using a long-pile roller. The rich velvety finish, reminiscent of a mossy green bank, is created by the subtle merging of colors. I placed spots of blue and green paints in the roller tray and lightly rollerpainted them onto the wall. When the first coat was dry, I placed spots of different shades of blue and green in the tray and rollerpainted them onto the wall in the same way.

Using rollers

Compared to using brushes, using rollers is a relatively new way of applying paint, so it is only in recent years that people have started to develop new ways of working with them.

Both sponge and long-pile rollers, with an uneven covering of paint, can be lightly applied to a surface to produce a mottled, textured effect, which varies according to the amount of pressure exerted and the number of layers applied. A long-pile roller leaves splodgy patches of paint while a sponge roller gives a finer look, although the end of the roller can leave lines.

1 Pour a little paint into a roller tray. Roll the roller into the paint, moving it up and down the tray to get a light but slightly uneven distribution of paint. The trick is not to saturate the roller. Lightly roll the roller across the surface, taking care not to press too hard; the idea is to keep a thin layer of paint through which you can still see the base color.

2 You can choose to work the roller in all directions or only horizontally and vertically, depending on the desired effect. Always let the first rollered color dry completely before applying another coat.

Crackle varnish

A crackled texture breaks up what could be an overly flat effect when working with natural colors such as grays, creams, and whites, and crackle varnish produces a sparse and minimal yet complex decoration. Look at the broken earth in a dried-up riverbed, the awesome and spare beauty of the crazed shapes formed by the arid mud, or visualize the fine mesh of delicate cracks on a piece of Japanese raku pottery, and you are imagining the effects you can imitate with the crackle varnish medium.

The special two-part medium is applied over a painted base coat, and, as the two mediums dry and react with one another, large or fine cracks appear in the surface. These cracks can then be filled with a color of your choice, for extra depth and accentuation.

There are various two-part kits on the market: here, we have used two water-based products. You can buy kits that determine the size of the cracks—large or small—although a more generous coat of the second medium usually results in larger cracks than a thin coat.

1 First coat your surface with a matte paint (see page 14). Use a fine, soft varnish brush to apply the first varnish-like medium, covering with an even, not too thin coat. To be sure you have covered the surface completely, it is a good idea to apply a second layer of this medium.

2 Follow your product's instructions before applying the second medium: some kits require the first coat to be completely dry, others only tacky. Apply the second medium generously, but not thickly, and leave to dry. The cracks begin to appear as the medium dries, but you can help it along by using a hair drier—set to low heat—or a heater.

3 When the crackle medium is dry and the cracks have fully developed, use artist's oil paint, not a water-based paint, to fill in the cracks. Use your finger or some paper towel to rub the paint all over the surface, pushing it into the cracks. Rub a little mineral spirits into the oil paint on the surface to dilute it and spread it out. Then use a wet sponge to wipe away the excess paint on the surface, leaving color in the cracks only. Varnish the finished effect with an oil-based varnish (see page 122).

Opposite: Looking like a fossilized dinosaur egg, this oval table is painted with a cracked effect over a warm gray-brown base. Some of the cracks are large while others are fine and densely-packed, giving a varied quality across the whole area. Fill the cracks with raw umber artist's oil paint to produce a creamy brown effect.

More ideas

Patination techniques work very well when combined with patterns. Circles, crescent shapes, or more intricate reverse stencils gain particular depth when executed over a textured background, while stripes or squares filled in with a patina have quite a different look to flat, solid painted shapes. The combination of flat color and textured patina has a special impact.

You can also try the patination techniques with different paints, such as glossy translucent or pearlized paint, for dramatic or subtle results.

Left: First paint the wall with brilliant yellow medium-luster paint (see page 21), then gently colorwash (see page 108) with a deep, burnt orange. Stick huge leaf shapes cut from paper over the dry colorwash, then work a darker second colorwash over the walls and the cutouts. The cutouts act as reverse stencils (see page 86) and when removed reveal the first colorwash.

Above left: A simple single frottage on this kitchen wall works well with the stainless steel accessories found elsewhere in the room. Over the gray-green wall I applied a blue frottage (see page 112), for a soft effect that does not interfere with the workings of the room.

Left: A small statue of Buddha sits calmly in front of a wild sea of turquoise-blue. Apply turquoise glossy glaze paint (see page 26) mixed with glaze (see page 121) over a brownish-purple medium-luster base (see page 21), to produce a rich, shiny finish which here enhances the gold of the statue. Wipe a cloth into the mixture in circles and arcs like clouds, sky, or wind.

Above: The decoration on this tabletop is inspired by the purple and blue of granite and slate. Paint the surface with a deep purple medium-luster paint (see page 21). First frottage (see page 112) a mid-blue glaze then, when dry, repeat the frottage technique with a light blue glaze.

Glossary

Acrylic size: see *water-based size.*

Acrylic varnish: see *varnish.*

Aluminum leaf: imitation silver *metal leaf.*

Artist's brushes: specialist paintbrushes in varying sizes and shapes. Use to freehand paint different brushmarks.

Artist's oil paint: thick, oil-based paint, predominantly used by artists. Rub dark oil paint into the cracks made by *crackle varnish.*

Base coat: first coat of paint, applied before a specialist paint or under a decorative technique. When working with *glaze,* a *medium-luster* base coat is best.

Brass leaf: imitation gold *metal leaf.*

Bronze powders: metallic powders available in many shades. Use with *water-based size* as a substitute for *metal leaf.*

Colored glaze: see *glaze.*

Colorizer: highly concentrated color used for coloring *glaze* or increasing the intensity of paint.

Comb: toothed instrument pulled through colored *glaze* to produce stripes. Buy a commercial rubber comb or make your own using cardboard.

Continental paintbrush: oval-shaped paintbrush that holds a generous amount of paint or *glaze.*

Copper leaf: *metal leaf* made from copper.

Craft knife: very sharp knife with replaceable blades. Use to cut card *stencils.*

Crackle varnish: commercial two-part product that produces a cracked effect.

Dragging brush: coarse, long-bristled brush pulled through colored *glaze* to produce very fine stripes.

Dutch metal leaf: alternative name for *brass leaf.*

Eggshell: particular type of *medium-luster paint.* Water-based varieties are easiest to use and can be mixed with water-based paints, *glazes,* and *varnishes.*

Emulsion/latex: water-based decorator's paint, usually with a *matte* or *medium-luster* finish.

Frottage: random, textured effect created by rubbing

Glaze: colorless, slow-drying translucent medium to which color is added in the form of paint. Apply colored glaze over a *base coat* and manipulate it, while still wet, using various tools–brushes, *combs,* cardboard, newspaper –to produce a pattern that reveals the base color in places. If you make a mistake, simply wipe the wet glaze away and begin again.

Oil- and water-based glazes are available but we only use water-based products in this book: they are easy to use, do not have strong odors, and brushes and tools are easily washed in water after use. Water-based glaze appears white in the container but dries to a semi-transparent finish.

To color water-based glaze, simply add water-based paint or colorizer. Pour the glaze into a roller tray and slowly add the paint, mixing it in with a spoon or paintbrush. The more paint added the darker the color will be and the quicker the glaze will dry. Precolored glaze is also available.

Gloss: paint with high-gloss finish. Water-based varieties are easiest to use and can be mixed with other water-based paints, *glazes,* and *varnishes.*

Glossy glaze paint: very shiny, translucent water-based paint. Apply with a brush or roller, overlapping paints to create new colors.

Gold leaf: sheets of real gold *metal leaf. Brass leaf* is a very effective, cheaper alternative.

Gold size: see *water-based size.*

Long-pile roller: paint roller made from a fluffy, woolly substance such as sheepskin (mohair). Use for a mottled finish. Use large rollers on walls and small rollers to paint stripes or for stenciling.

Masking tape: self-adhesive tape. Use to mask areas you do not want to paint, especially when painting lines. Always buy a low-tack variety, as this can be removed without damaging surfaces.

Matte paint: water-based paint with a flat finish.

Medium-luster paint: water-based paint with a finish between *gloss* and *matte.* Available with varying degrees

121

of sheen. See also *eggshell* and *satin latex,* also called semi-gloss.

Metal leaf: wafer-thin sheets of beaten metal. Apply to any surface using *water-based size.* Real gold and silver leaf are available but the cheaper alternatives–*brass and aluminum*–are excellent substitutes. Copper and distressed-effect sheets are also available.

Metallic paint: water-based paint with a high gloss in metallic finishes such as gold, silver, and copper.

Patina: surface film or texture, usually produced by age.

Patterned roller: rubber roller covered in raised nodules, usually used for making decorative effects in plaster. Use with paint to produce thousands of tiny spots.

Pearlized paint: reflective, gloss paint that changes in appearance with changing light. The pearly effect is reminiscent of the inside of an oyster's shell. Paints appear white in the container and the color they dry to depends on the intensity of the *base coat* color.

Pigment: coloring matter used in paint. Powder pigments are available from art supply stores. Use them to color *polished plaster* and *varnish.*

Plumb line: weighted string. Attach to the wall to mark straight verticals when painting stripes.

Polished plaster: colored, shiny plaster made from marble dust, lime, cement, and *pigment.* Apply the plaster with a trowel and polish it with the edge of the trowel to produce a shine.

Polyurethane varnish: see *varnish.*

Reverse stencil: solid shape cut from card or paper to block out paint. Apply paint around the edges of the shape, then remove the stencil to reveal the shape depicted in the base color.

Sandpaper: abrasive paper available in varying degrees of coarseness. Use to make a smooth surface.

Satin latex: type of water-based *medium-luster paint.*

Scumble: another name for *glaze.*

Silver leaf: sheets of real silver *metal leaf. Aluminum leaf* is a very effective, cheaper alternative.

Size: see *water-based size.*

Sparkle paint: minute flecks of glitter held in a transparent liquid. The color of the sparkles in the paint are

affected by the *base coat* color and the changing light.

Spirit level: glass tube partly filled with spirit: the position of the air bubble indicates horizontality. Use to mark straight lines on a wall.

Sponge roller: paint roller made from sponge. Use for a smooth, flat finish. Large rollers are available for use on walls while smaller rollers can be used to paint stripes or for stenciling.

Spray repositioning glue: spray adhesive that allows you to remove or reposition paper or card. Use for attaching *stencils.*

Stamp: shaped object covered with paint and applied to the surface to leave a printed impression. Many household objects are used as stamps: potatoes, plastic cups, sponges.

Steel wool: abrasive material, available in varying degrees of coarseness. Use to rub back paintwork.

Stencil: shape or motif cut out of card. Apply paint with a brush or roller through the cutout shape.

Stencil card: specialist thin, strong card used specifically for making *stencils.* Everyday thin cardboard can also be used.

Stippling brush: square brush with flat, boxlike bristles. Work the brush into colored *glaze* to produce millions of tiny dots.

Tone: term used to describe how dark or light a color is. Different colors can be the same tone.

Varnish: transparent protective medium. Apply over your decoration to ensure long-term protection from scuffs and scratches and prevent colors fading. Varnishes are available in matte, medium-luster and gloss finishes. Water-based varnish, also known as acrylic varnish, is odorless, colorless, and quick–drying. Oil-based varnish, also known as polyurethane varnish, is strong and, when dry, imparts a yellow tone to the decoration. Varnish can be colored with *pigments.* Apply any varnish using a *varnish brush.*

Varnish brush: flat-ended brush with long bristles. Use to apply *varnish.*

Wallpaper paste: thick glue. Use to fix paper shapes to a surface. The shapes can be removed easily at a later date by dampening the paper.

Water-based glaze: see *glaze.*

Water-based size: specialist glue used to adhere *metal leaf* and *bronze powders.*

Suppliers

Below is a list of suppliers, listed alphabetically. Annie Sloan products are available by mail order by calling the Annie Sloan order line at +44 870 601 0082, or her distributors as below. Details of products can be found on Annie's internet site at www.anniesloan.com and Annie can also be contacted by e-mail at paint@anniesloan.com.

Bestt Liebco Corporation
1201 Jackson Street
Philadelphia, Pennsylvania 19148
Toll-Free 1-800-523-9095
Fax (215) 463-0988
Email ‹bestliebco@aol.com›
Manufactures wide variety of specialty brushes for paint effects, including mottlers, softeners, stipplers, sponges, floggers, blenders, and splatter brushes. Contact for local retailer.

Briwax Woodcare Products
220 South Main Street
Auburn, Maine 04210
Toll-Free 1-800- 274-9299
24 hr Fax Line (212) 504 9550
Email ‹Information@BriwaxWoodcare.com›
http://www.BriwaxWoodcare.com
Shellacs and varnishes.

Firenz Enterprises, Inc.
12976 SW 132 Avenue
Miami, Florida 33186
Tel (305) 232-0233 Fax (305) 232-3191
E-Mail ‹Firenze@gateway.net›
http://www.rivesto-marmorino.com
Distributor of Rivesto-Marmorino (marble dust plaster) in 27 premixed colors, plus Italian-made trowels.

Golden Artist Colors, Inc
188 Bell Road
New Berlin, New York 13411-9527
Toll-Free 1-888-397-2468
Tel (607) 847-6154 Fax (607) 847-6767
Email ‹orderinfo@goldenpaints.com›
http://www.goldenpaints.com
Artists' acrylic paints, retardants, mediums, and varnishes.

HK Holbein
Box 555, 20 Commerce Street
Williston, Vermont 05495
Toll-Free 1-800-682-6686
Tel (802) 862-4573 Fax (802) 658-5889
1751 Richardson Street, #2111
Montreal, Quebec H3K 1G6
Toll-Free 1-800-361-7581
Tel (514) 933-4019 Fax (514) 933-0389
http://www.holbeinhk.com
Worldwide supplier of fine art and craft supplies.

Homestead House Authentic Milk Paint
95 Niagara Street
Toronto, Ontario M5V 1C3
Tel (416) 504-9984
Distributor of paint products including milk paint. Call for color samples.

Kremer Pigments Inc.
228 Elizabeth Street
New York, New York 10012
Tel (212) 219-2394 Fax (212) 219-2394
http://www.kremer-pigmente.de
German-made cadmium pigments, natural earth and iron oxide pigments, metal powders, pearl luster pigments, powdered stains, organic dyes.

The Old Fashioned Milk Paint Co., Inc.
436 Main Street
Groton, Massachusetts 01450
Tel (978) 448-6336
http://www.milkpaint.com
Powdered milk paint in a wide range of historical colors.

Paint and Decorating Retailers Association
403 Axminister Drive
St. Louis, Missouri 63026-2941
Tel (636) 326-2636 Fax (636) 326-1823
http://www.pdra.org
Trade association of paint and decorating stores in U.S. and Canada. On-line directory of member retailers.

Paint Effects
2426 Fillmore Street
San Francisco, Califiornia 94115
Tel (415) 292-7780 Fax (415) 292-7782
http://www.painteffects.com
Quality decorative paint and stenciling supplies, including Annie Sloan Pigments, glazing liquid in 20 colors, oil- and water-based craquelure, decoupage lacquer, varnishing and antiquing waxes, liming paste, brushes and tools. Wide selection of stencils and decoupage drawings imported from UK and Canada.

Paint Magic Mail Order
412 Pebble Creek Court
Pennington, New Jersey 08534
Toll-Free 1-877-330-0445
Fax (609) 737-7333
Email <PntMgc@aol.com>
http://www.desmondint.com/PaintMagic
Prepared paint solutions including colorwash, emulsions, scumble glaze, craqueleure, patina, impasto, limewash, marmorino, primers, distemper, and suede paint. Canadian orders call for details.

Paris Paint Techniques
Valerie Traynor
91 Rutland Street
Carlisle, Massachusetts 01741
Tel (978) 369-3440
Email <paristrayn@aol.com>
Distributor and stockist of complete range of Annie Sloan Paints.

Pearl Paints
308 Canal Street
New York, New York 10013
U.S. Toll-Free 1-800-221-6845   x2297
International (212) 431-7932   x2297
http://www.pearlpaint.com
Paints and fine art supplies, including speckle paints, textured gels, Sennelier dry pigments, gold leaf.

Periwinkle Essential Stencils
P.O. Box 457
West Kennebunk, Maine 04094
Tel (207) 985-8020 Fax (207) 985-1601
Email <periwinkle@cybertours.com>
http://www.cybertours.com/periwinkle/home.html
Stencil patterns include botanical paintings, Delft pottery, and William Morris designs.

Pierre Finkelstein Institute of Decorative Painting, Inc.
20 West 20th Street, Suite 1009
New York, New York 10011
Toll-Free 1-888-328-9278
http://www.pfinkelstein.com
European specialty brushes by mail order.

Porter's Original Paints
Sydney, Australia
Tel (818) 623-9394 Fax (818) 623-9210
http://www.porters.com.au
Lime wash, French wash, milk paint, wood wash, distemper, fresco, liquid copper and patina green, liquid iron and instant rust, Roman cement. U.S. office ships to Canada.

R&F Handmade Paints, Inc.
110 Prince Street
Kingston, New York 12401
Toll-Free 1-800-206-8088
Tel (914) 331-3112 Fax (914) 331-3242
Email <mail@RFPaints.com>
http://www.rfpaints.com
Handmade paints – pigment sticks and encaustics. On-line retail locator.

Sepp Leaf Products, Inc.
381 Park Avenue South
New York, NY 10016
Toll-Free 1-800-971-7377
Tel (212) 683-2840 Fax (212) 725-0308
Email <sales@seppleaf.com>
http://www.seppleaf.com
Gold and metal leaf from Italy, Germany, France, Japan and China, plus supplies and tools. Liberon gilding, wood finishing and restoration products. Kolcaustico venetian plaster.

Sharon Matas
309 Earles Lane
Newton Square, Philadelphia 19073
Tel (610) 396-4952
Distributor and stockist of a complete range of Annie Sloan Paints.

Sinopia LLC
229 Valencia Street
San Francisco, California 94103
Tel (415) 621-2898 Fax (415) 621 2897
http://www.sinopia.com
Kremer Pigments plus metal powders and filings, mica flakes for sparkle effects, bronzing powders, colored marble dust from Italy, Venetian plaster, gilding materials, specialty brushes, shellacs, waxes and varnishes, acrylic glazing liquids.

Stampers Studio
2255A Queen Street East
Toronto, Ontario
Tel (416) 690-4446 Fax (416) 690-7131
http://www.the-beaches.com/stampers
Extensive range of stamps.

Surface Solutions
2018 Ranleigh Avenue
Toronto, Ontario M4N 1W9
Tel (416) 488-6404
Distributor of Algalite Venetian Plaster and plaster supplies used throughout Italy to restore public monuments and buildings.

Index

Acknowledgments & Credits

Author's acknowledgments

This book, like all books, is the result of the combined effort of many people. I would like to thank Kate Kirby, Claire Waite, Jonathan Raimes and Tino Tedaldi for all their various talents which have helped make this book.

Special thanks to Philip Bailey for his expert help and patient guidance with polished plasters, pages 48–53.

I am also very grateful to Jason Arbuckle, David and Hester Lott, Claire Waite and Andrew Brown, Sarah and Tino Tedaldi, and Daniela and Jonathan Raimes for allowing us to photograph their homes.

Thanks also to the following for lending objects used for photography:

PAGE 49 BOTTOM LEFT
Sophie Cook
Waterside Studios, 99 Rotherhithe Street,
London SE16 4NF
Tel: +44 20 7394 3241

PAGE 53 BOTTOM RIGHT
Max Lamb and Fiona Wilkes Glass Design, Waterside Studios, 99 Rotherhithe Street, London SE16 4NF
Tel: +44 20 7237 5630

PAGE 52
Stuart Möller
Waterside Studios, 99 Rotherhithe Street,
London SE16 4NF
Tel: +44 797 4850339

PAGE 41
Carol Wainwright
Represented by Oxford Gallery, Oxford, England

PAGE 39
Steve Newell (white glass jug)
Majolica Works (blue jug)
Catherine Hargh (glass vase)
All represented by Oxford Gallery, Oxford, England

Visit Annie Sloan's website for advice on materials and to view the online catalog.
Get answers to your decorating questions.

website: www.anniesloan.com
e-mail: paint@anniesloan.com

Picture Credits

The photographs on these pages appear by kind permission of the following sources:

Christie's Images: 49 top right (© Kate Rothko Prizel and Christopher Rothko/DACS, 2000), 95 top left (© Ars, N.Y. and DACS, London, 2000)

Jérome Darblay & Charles Rutherford: 53 top left, 129 top left

Edifice Picture Library: 13 top left, 18 top right and bottom right, 25 top left, bottom left and right, 37 top right and bottom right, 49 top left, 69 bottom right, 106 top right and bottom left

Garden Picture Library: 57 top left

Carol Kane: 9 below, 13 top right and bottom right, 30 top left, bottom left and right, 37 bottom left, 42 top left and right, bottom left, 49 bottom right, 56 bottom left, 69 top left and right, 82 bottom right, 95 bottom right

Kim Sayer: 82 top left, 106 top left

Science Photo Library: 8 top left, 9 bottom right, 56 top left and right, 95 bottom left

Geoff Dann 51 bottom left, 52-53